OUR potpourri PLANET

First published in 2025 by HarperCollins *Publishers* India
4th Floor, Tower A, Building No. 10, DLF Cyber City,
DLF Phase II, Gurugram, Haryana — 122002
www.harpercollins.co.in

2 4 6 8 10 9 7 5 3 1

P-ISBN: 978-93-6569-420-8
E-ISBN: 978-93-6569-233-4

Ranjit Lal asserts the moral right
to be identified as the author of this work.

The views and opinions expressed in this book are the author's own
and the facts, verified to the extent possible, are as reported by him.
The publishers are not in any way liable for the same. The illustrations
are an artistic representation of the creatures and events described
and are not meant to be scientific depictions.

Inside illustrations, design and typeset: Anushua Sinha
Cover art and design: Anushua Sinha

Typeset in DrescherGroteskBTW01-Book

Printed and bound at
Nutech Print Services - India

🇫🇮🇩🇮🅾️✖️ HarperCollinsIn

This book is printed on FSC® certified paper
which ensures responsible forest management.

OUR Potpourri PLANET

Ranjit Lal

Illustrated by
Anushua Sinha

HarperCollins *Publishers* India

CONTENTS

Part II

Part III

OUR PRECIOUS POTPOURRI PLANET: INTRODUCTION

W hen the suggestion was first put to me that I do a book on climate change, global warming and the environment, I recoiled as if I had touched a live wire. No way! I get three newspapers a day and if that isn't bad enough, watch nature programs on TV, which these days are either full of blood and gore, or tell grim, doomsday-predicting horror stories about how the end is nigh and how our kids and grandkids are going to hate and damn us forever.

But my agent, Jaya Bhattacharji Rose, persisted. 'They want a positive spin on the book; it has to be optimistic,' she said, and I kind of rolled my eyes. Besides I didn't have any formal degree or training in the environmental sciences, nor had I spent twenty years tramping about in the rainforests of the Western Ghats, or the Eastern Himalayas, studying elephants, frogs or fungi. My forays into the wild have been few and far between; I've lived in big, bustling, very polluted cities all my life. Due to health issues, I was not allowed to trek and had a ceiling of 6,000 feet. So, what did I have to show and tell?

Slowly, ideas started filtering in. And then it became an avalanche of material barging into my head, like people trying to get on a Mumbai local on Monday morning. What about that bird dropping that suddenly came alive? Or that spider that had cunningly built her web smack on the highway that ants used, pouncing on at least one every day? Had she done a recce before setting her trap? Or that paradise flycatcher which I tried to photograph standing knee-deep in garbage? Or how I had become interested in birds in the first place? Or, in fact, how I had become interested in nature in the first place? And why? And why the heck are we going around like lunatics, mucking up all the world's most beautiful wild places, dumping crap into our oceans and pumping poisonous fumes into our skies, like there is no tomorrow? We're choking up and inexorably cooking our planet, which does not augur well for the future. At the rate at which we're going, there could well be no tomorrow.

One advantage I had is that while I was growing up there was, for the most part, no TV and absolutely no Internet or social media (it could take eight years to get a big black rotary dial Bakelite telephone). But there was a huge, wild garden in Madras (now Chennai), where we lived for five years when I was a child, and where, on holidays, I rode roughshod nearly the whole day on my bike. I knew squat about nature, but I did know which ants would bite you and which were friendly. I also knew to quickly back away from the rafts of fierce chilli-red ants that drifted towards you in flooded sections of the garden during the monsoon, lest they swarm up your shorts. (My sister tells me that she hasn't forgotten the boils she got from wading in that dirty rainwater!) And that it was very foolish to poke a stick into a wasp's nest, and that the little fish that lived in the well outside our verandah were not interested in attah balls attached to bent paper clips. That it was fun to tickle a grasshopper or a frog so that it would zing or hopscotch away and watch the friendly-eyed geckos stalk and pounce on moths as cunningly as any panther. That the sticky umber-brown tamarinds that you gathered from under the tree were more delicious than boiled sweets. That it was fun to shoot down a raw mango from a tree, and have it with red chilli powder, nimbu juice and chaat masala. And of course that, when you climbed trees, you did not fall out of them.

Then, when I was ten, we moved to Bombay (now Mumbai), which even then (1965) was claustrophobic, and didn't have the wild rambling gardens and spaces I was used to. But it did have the Borivali National Park, where Mumbai's lakes, Tulsi, Vihar and Powai, glimmered like dark mirrors of mercury in the monsoons, and where the foliage was emerald and rampant. Reputedly there were crocodiles in the lakes and leopards in the forest. (The latter certainly are still there, prowling about looking for dogs.) We picnicked here regularly and it was here that I was entranced by my first glimpse of grey hornbills, squealing like rusted machinery as they flew across an iron sky, looking as antediluvian as anything out of *Jurassic Park*. My friends and I would even bunk college to drive to the park; on early mornings we had to wake up the guard to open the barriers.

Then there was the Marve beach, where I used to spend weekends and which, in those days, was nearly deserted. Beaches are the sort of places where you can really let your imagination (and dog) off the leash and think silly (or deep) poetic thoughts!

(No, no, both are good for you!) Sadly, I still knew squat about the fascinating creatures that scuttled and scurried along the tidelines. I did know you had to avoid the glistening purple and green Portuguese man o' war that studded the beach during the monsoon. But it was hugely exhilarating walking along the varnished beach with the wind buffeting you in the back and the ferocious rollers booming and exploding into shrapnel on the jagged rocks, where huge green-black crabs clattered at each other. The little sand-coloured crabs would bamboozle Bambi, our Boxer, by doing a little shimmy under her nose and vanishing, even as she frowned at them and tried digging them out. Raindrops, fat and silver, like airgun pellets would smack into your face, driven by the raucous briny breeze. And later there was always fresh prawn curry and rice, not to mention chilled beer!

I had for the most part ignored birds – as far as I was concerned, they were just darting black specks in the sky, until it was suggested by friends that I look at them a little closer. So, I bought myself a pair of giant 10X50 Zenith binoculars and focused on the first bird I could spot on the peepul tree outside our fourth-floor balcony in Mumbai. It looked like a clown! It was dumpy, small as a sparrow, a leafy green and streaky off-white with a face done up in crimson, yellow and black. It had huge kohl-lined eloquent black eyes. It was standing on tiptoe, facing first one way and then the other – and hiccupping! 'Tok-tok-tok!' Gin first thing in the morning, eh? Good on you! Well, I thought happily, if the very first bird I had spotted looked like an inebriated clown, what the hell did the other 1,300 or so birds in our country look like? I hold that coppersmith responsible for all that followed.

Of course, there were the few and far-between trips to sanctuaries and national parks. But always just being there, for me at least, seemed far more important than what I saw there. On one trip to Kalagarh near Corbett I spent more time being mesmerized by emerald and black damselflies dancing over the smooth grey and maroon river rocks than in looking for tiger pugmarks. I still haven't seen a tiger in the wild and I'm afraid the lions at Gir were no compensation: they were just so blasé about us (even unashamedly having a honeymoon right in front of us, moral police be damned!) that they seemed tame. (Don't let that fool you for a second — they'll swipe off your face if you try to take a selfie with them!)

There were also precious holidays at hill stations, where again birds and creepy-crawlies became the centre of my attention. On one ten-day trip to Palampur I spent most of my time knee-deep in wet grass trying to photograph paradise flycatchers, who would whistle me out of the house and then give me the royal run-around all morning! On another holiday in Naukuchiyatal I stationed myself in the midst of the resort's garbage dump, waiting for the same birds. (This made perfect sense — paradise flycatchers live up to their name and catch flies, so what better place than in a garbage dump in paradise?) And then there were the great mountains, of course — glittering like cracked cutglass in the distance, floating halfway up in the sky, wearing cloaks of snow on their sides and down in their valleys.

So, I think Mother Nature has a very cunning trick (among her millions of tricks) up her sleeve: Look at her for a bit, check things out and she will begin to draw you in, like a gravitational force. If you are a normal human being, questions will begin to surface in your head like dolphins popping their heads out of the water to say hello. Why, when, where, how? And then, like a purebred nosy-parker, you will start to search for answers, most of which these days, thanks to the Great God Google and the vast amount of available literature on the net, you can find quite easily (But do crosscheck your sources!). And some of those answers — many of them, in fact — can be completely mind-blowing! Mother Nature has a gazillion million gobsmacking miracles in her treasure chest, with so many still to be discovered. Perhaps one of the most important stems from what so many astronauts have said as they orbit the Earth. That our small blue, green and white, potpourri planet is by far the most beautiful thing they have ever set their eyes on. And that we have probably used up all our luck ever since the Big Bang 13.8 billion years ago, and which later formed the Earth 4.5 billion years back, in that it orbits in that narrow, blessed band in the solar system, where you would neither burn up, nor become a solid block of ice. And most importantly, where the miracle of life was conjured up, some 2.4 billion years ago, which now has evolved and diversified into a million gazillion forms from invisible single-cell organisms, bacteria and viruses to blue whales and giant redwoods, all working diligently to ensure the survival and propagation of their genes and, in doing so, of each other, and of life on earth. All of which are now sadly under dire threat by our wayward, wastrel ways, which is not making Mother Nature a happy camper; she is getting rather hot under the collar and has begun throwing tantrums.

So, what did we do to make her so annoyed? So annoyed that we're now being warned that we've screwed up enough, so much that she's begun striking back in ways we just won't be able to handle. So annoyed that if we go on like this, our precious potpourri planet will sooner rather than later come apart at the seams and be unlivable. So yes, while Mother Nature knew how to balance her books to ensure that life went on, in spite of the odd temper tantrum she might have thrown in the past millions of years, she probably didn't account for us: the most 'successful' form of life she was responsible for evolving. In any case, the last five occasions when life was in danger of going extinct (aka 'the five great extinctions') on planet Earth were due to geological, seismic, meteorological and even interstellar space events (like that rogue meteorite that didn't look where it was heading and smashed into the Earth 65.5 million years ago, causing the great dinosaurs to go extinct). This time, it is we who are being held responsible because of our activities, which over just the last 250+ years have brutalized and disfigured the Earth as never before and uncorked the greenhouse gas genie out of its bottle, unable to put it back in again.

It started off with the invention of the steam engine in the latter half of the eighteenth century, which put mechanical power into our hands like never before. But steam power was just the starter, and led the way to the Industrial and Energy Revolutions which transformed life on earth forever. Experts now say that the middle of the twentieth century was when the balloon really went up (and call this the age of the Anthropocene) when oil-, gas- and coal-powered gigantic factories and manufacturing units began mass production. The burning of these fossil fuels in the manufacturing process, for transport and heating, let loose vast amounts of carbon dioxide, water vapour, methane and other noxious greenhouse gases into the atmosphere at a level never experienced before. For 800,000 years before the Industrial Revolution, there were a around 250 parts of carbon dioxide for every million air molecules. In 2022, this figure was a staggering 421 parts per million. All those greenhouse gases being vented has led to a rise in global temperatures: on land, in the seas and most critically at the poles. We're trying to control the rise to 1.5 degrees Celsius by 2100 but it looks like we're going to overshoot that quite considerably; some say it's going to be warmer by between 2 and 4 degrees Celsius. And the consequences of that are going to be catastrophic.

The Industrial Revolution fed off itself: as populations exploded, so did demand for food and goods. Mass production enabled goods to be produced at lower and lower prices, leading to the rise of consumer societies in what were being called the developed countries (often at the cost of the countries they colonized and whose resources they looted). And in all the heady joy of being able to buy cheap shiny new cars every year, cheap gas and petrol, cheap electricity, all the white goods we could ever dream of and 1,500 breakfast cereals to choose from, we ignored something vital: that, like it or not, or believe it or not, we were still dependent on fungi, bacteria, green plants, trees, forests, insects, reptiles, fishes, amphibians, birds and mammals and most importantly, the places where they lived (their habitats), to run the earth on an even keel. That by gouting great volumes of greenhouse gases, by felling and drowning vast swathes of rainforests, and gouging gargantuan areas of the earth for metals, minerals, coal and oil, by all our unbridled and destructive activities, we were making it increasingly difficult for this great earth 'maintenance crew' to continue its work — sustaining life (including ours) on the planet. More about such activities in a later chapter.

Over the last 2.4 billion years, Mother Nature has evolved myriad specialist and generalist forms of life (her maintenance crew) to perform this task; many have come and gone and been replaced, a process that still goes on. In Part I of the book, we meet just a sampling of her astonishments — some which I have personal experience of, and others which I wish I did. And most of which we have found out about by being the most inquisitive nosy-parkers to have ever roamed the planet. Hopefully, this should make you put away your computer game, turn off your smartphone and go do a hike in the nearest wilderness or city park! The more of this treasure trove of a planet you become aware of, discover and explore, the more likely you are to be horrified by what we're doing to it. And hopefully this will make it your life's ambition to try to ensure that these wondrous treasures and creatures remain safe and healthy in the habitats they call home: collectively, our precious potpourri Planet Earth.

Part II takes a look at the results of our activities: at the guillotine that's poised over myriad species that share the planet with us and that has already fallen on so many. It looks at the temper tantrums Mother Nature has thrown in response, the warnings she has given us, of what climate change and global warming is going to mean for and do to us as she vents her fury via floods, wildfires, droughts, thundering tornadoes and storms, heatwaves, landslides, rising sea levels, massive erosion, et al.

Way back in 1962, Bob Dylan wrote his iconic 'A Hard Rain's A-Gonna Fall' in response to the Cold War between the then Soviet Union and the United States. It's a very different war we are fighting today, but the lyrics of that song are equally relevant now as they were then. 'I heard the sound of a thunder, it roared out a warnin'/ Heard the roar of a wave that could drown the whole world…' We'd better take heed of that thunder and listen to that roar. There are unprecedented floods, raging infernos, sizzling heatwaves, massive die-outs that are already happening, and are now threatening to get out of control. (Some cheerful folks think things are already out of control.)

This section also takes a look at some of our 'sins of omission and commission'. Where we have deliberately ignored old wisdom that taught us how to live with nature rather than fight against her (and there can only be one winner and it's not us); how so many nations have bulldozed and bayoneted their way into once self-sustaining habitats, pillaged local people's ecosystems, uprooted their ways of life, and polluted and looted the air, water and land in order to become 'wealthy'.

Ah, you might think, this is all going downhill very rapidly. But wait. Part III throws light on what we are doing to try to cool Big Mama down so that she doesn't totally flush us down the toilet in the near future. Most countries in the world have now realized that 'Hey Houston, we have a problem!' and are making attempts to come together, to course correct — setting targets and making rules via global institutions. Many governments are doing the same thing, though sadly there are too many leaders who say (and promise) one thing and do and deliver just the opposite, and which I think are the most insidious and dangerous of them all. But there are also thousands of organizations, NGOs and ordinary people like you and me all over the world, who have really given their all to the cause, often with heart-lifting results and impacts. Frankly, at this stage we need everyone to be like them: if they can create forests out of wastelands, why can't we? If one young man (Afroz Shah) can start a movement to clean up Mumbai's filthy beaches, why can't we do something similar? If a couple of Balinese preteen sisters, Melati and Isabel Wijsen, just ten and twelve years old when they started, can eventually force (by going on a hunger strike!) their government to ban the use of plastic bags on their island, why can't we do something similar in our own neck of the woods? Happily, there are thousands of such examples: drops in the ocean you might think, but then the ocean is made out of drops.

But first let's take a look at some of the wonders of our potpourri planet, of the creatures, big and small, which have worked together and made this a place we all can call 'home'... our precious potpourri Planet Earth.

A NOTE ON CRAZY NUMBER CRUNCHING

All the statistics and numbers quoted in this book have been taken from sources which appeared as 'reliable' (as journalists like to say) as I believed them to be at the time when I met them.

But reader beware! Every time I rechecked a batch of numbers I'd land up with a set of different figures! Statistics seem to be very dynamic and, depending on your source, may differ significantly. In this book, please treat them as indicative and not gospel. In fact, it would be fun to look up the numbers yourself and arrive at your own conclusions!

One major and alarming conclusion I arrived at was that how little we really seem to know. No one can categorically claim accuracy for varying reasons.

1: It may be obviously impossible to count, say, the exact number of spiders in the world today. Statisticians all have their various formulae for estimating these figures and you can be sure statistician A will disagree vehemently with statistician B's methodology/formula in doing so. Or even if both methods of calculating data may be sound and valid, they may just be throwing up different results — statistical democracy at work!

2: Sources may have their own private agendas. For example, the officials in Sariska Tiger Reserve for several years claimed that according to their census records the number of tigers in the park were increasing year on year. When in fact that number turned out to be zero! Government sources may claim that only 1,000 trees are to be cut for a major dam project; an NGO on the ground may say that figure is 100,000! And neither you nor I can personally go and count all the trees in that location to verify the figures.

3: There's always competition between different sources: ah, we have worse news to give than you do, so listen to us! You say that the world will end by 2100; according to us, it's going to end in 2050! (This also happens with the news media when they give you the death toll after, say, a natural disaster.)

But statistics do point in a particular direction (usually pessimistic), which is their most important contribution. They show us trends — are there increases or decreases and, if so, by extrapolation what will they likely be in the future? But then, always remember that old cliché: there are lies, damn lies and statistics!

PART 1

The Wonder of It All

CHAPTER 1: GREEN MAGIC

W hile scientists are still trying to wrap their heads around (and furiously debating) the question of how exactly life on earth began, they and we do know about the ingenious plot Mother Nature hatched to ensure that it went on. The first order of the day, was of course, a reliable, steady source of energy to power up life with. Ah, there was the sun, just 93 million miles away, glowing generously and steadily and providing all the energy ever needed. But this energy, emitted in the form of photons (light), needed to be harnessed. So up she came with the idea of evolving a molecule — a rather large one — that could do just that: chlorophyll, which was a soothing green colour (because it reflected only green light) and which could be found in cyanobacteria (one of the pioneering photo synthesizers), green algae and green plants. Cyanobacteria, formerly known as blue-green algae, and a minute bacteria, were first off the blocks, photosynthesizing so efficiently that it produced so much oxygen that the era was called the 'great oxidation event'. Eventually oxygen levels stabilized, as much of the cyanobacteria died, but not before multi-cellular life evolved. After this, there was no looking back. It's thought the first 'animals' to emerge were sponges, some 800 million years ago, able to tolerate the now low oxygen levels in the oceans, and then first land plants about 470 million years ago, after which life forms went pretty berserk.

One Miracle Molecule

To provide sustenance and therefore energy for life, this miracle chlorophyll molecule absorbed carbon dioxide from the atmosphere and sucked up water and water vapor. Using the energy from the photons, chlorophyll split the water into hydrogen and oxygen atoms. It then used the hydrogen in combination with the carbon dioxide to manufacture sugars and carbohydrates, which powered life and enabled growth. The oxygen it kindly released back into the atmosphere — this was necessary to burn those sugars and carbs to produce the energy other living creatures need to walk and run and sing and dance, to be alive, to grow and to make more of ourselves! And brilliantly, every living breathing creature (and now, alas, too many non-breathing ones, like cars!) emitted the carbon dioxide so vitally needed by plants to live and grow. Which indeed they did, and became the source of our own sustenance, our fuel and food: fruit and vegetables, seeds, tubers and roots. Mammals, reptiles, amphibians, fish, insects — every living creature dined out on these to fuel their own bodies. Hardcore carnivores simply dined out deliciously on other animals which had become plump and juicy on a plant diet. So, in essence, we are all solar powered. Alas, we still can't manufacture our own food, so are dependent essentially on plants and the animals that eat those plants (and often each other). Can you imagine the number of Nobel Prizes a scientist would have deserved had they thought of an ideal way for humans to produce their own food? Okay, so Big Boss Mama Nature got there first, but we can and should use the principle and philosophy behind it – that what goes around comes around, that nothing goes to waste – in the way we live today. Because that is the only way that things can work out in the end.

We all know that leaves are the storehouses of chlorophyll and leaves grow on trees and bushes, which is why it's so important to have forests and green areas. In reality, around 50 per cent of the oxygen in the atmosphere is emitted by tiny plankton and other plants floating in the sea. But a good amount of this is used up by marine life and the decomposition that follows when these creatures die. But it's not all hunky-dory for green plants: their leaves have pores called stomata through which they release oxygen and absorb carbon dioxide. But they also lose water vapour through these same pores. In dry places this can be a problem for the plant, because it needs as much water as it can get. In humid, cool places, you may have noticed beads of moisture beautifully rimming a leaf (on days when there's no dew) in the morning; this is excess water that the leaf is getting rid of.

Neat, Eh?

Ah, I can hear the wheels in your brain whirr and see the gleam in your eye as you prepare to pounce! If there is more carbon dioxide in the air, won't that help plant life – and therefore us – to thrive? The plants will grow bigger and lusher, vegetarians and herbivores will have more to eat and get plumper and juicier, as will carnivores (and our burgers). Best of all, there'll be more oxygen to go around for everyone! So, theoretically, wouldn't cars and other carbon dioxide emitters actually help rather than hinder this process?

Well, for a start we are hacking down vast swathes of forest every second, reducing their capacity to produce oxygen. Also, we must remember that plants only work the day shift: at night, in the absence of light, they just breathe out carbon dioxide like all the rest of us, which is why we are told not to keep green plants in our bedrooms at night. So, if there's too much carbon dioxide around, we will all suffocate. The classic candle-in-a-jar experiment will reveal this: the candle needs oxygen to burn and once the oxygen is used up, pfft, the flame goes out! Yes, that's not likely to happen to you (unless you're locked in a car with the windows rolled up) because there's relatively little carbon dioxide in the atmosphere (compared to other gases). But carbon dioxide in collusion with water vapor and other greenhouse gases like ozone and methane acts like a kind of tea cosy over our potpourri planet, trapping and reflecting the heat generated and causing all sorts of problems in those areas of the planet that try to keep temperatures as steady as they can, such as ice caps and oceans. And with our millions of jets, cars, trains, massive power plants and factories producing everything from silicon chips to bulldozers by the million, all emitting carbon dioxide and other noxious gases in the process, we are physically heating up the planet too: for instance, as much as 60 per cent of the energy produced by an internal combustion engine dissipates as heat, only 30 per cent being used for actual propulsion. Every time anything is burnt it produces carbon dioxide and often other even more dreadful gases like carbon monoxide, nitrous oxides and methane. Most significantly, we get the fuel to burn in our factories and power our luxury cars and aircraft carriers from the fossilized remnants of plants that died millions of years ago, and were buried and compressed under considerable pressure, taking the carbon they contained with them. In three words: coal, gas and oil. We burn that coal, gas and oil and set that carbon free in the form of carbon dioxide.

Balancing Her Books

Mother Nature had balanced her equation beautifully. For life to go on serenely, she created an atmosphere consisting of about 20.9 per cent oxygen, 78 per cent nitrogen, around 0.93 per cent argon and just 0.04 per cent gases like carbon dioxide, methane and nitrous oxide. However, we have increased the amount of carbon dioxide in the atmosphere by a whopping 45 per cent since the start of the Industrial Age, disrupting the finely crafted balance. Carbon dioxide is a steady, heavy gas that can stick around for 300 to 1000 years without decomposing (unlike some of the other more unstable gases like methane and ozone). And Mother Nature is fiery, finicky and tempestuous; she doesn't like being messed around with, which is what we are doing and which is making her so cranky and unpredictable.

Hard Times

It has not been an easy ride for our planet, ever since her birth. Meteorites have hurtled into her, supervolcanoes have exploded every now and then, lava fields as large as continents have boiled and bubbled, tectonic plates have shifted and butted heads, her magnetic field has waxed and waned and even turned upside down, the seas have risen and fallen and she has been roasted and frozen in turn. In spite of this, life has somehow soldiered on. Oh yes, there have been monumental casualties along the way – mass annihilation and extinctions of entire species (the extinction of dinosaurs 66 million years ago being a classic) – and yet there have been survivors. While some of these incidents, such as the drifting of continents, have occurred over a period of millions of years, others, like the eruption of supervolcanoes such as Toba in Indonesia some 74,000 years ago, which some scientists theorize left just up to 10,000 human survivors on earth, had much more immediate as well as longer-lasting effects. There was a severe volcanic winter around the world for six to ten years after the blow up and a cooling phase that continued for the next 1,000 years. (I wonder if that's how the term 'toba-toba!' came about!)

At any rate, once the spark of life was lit and chlorophyll got its act going, life on earth kind of went berserk in spite of our planet being in a near-permanent state of post-traumatic stress disorder! It diversified and evolved rapidly in every which way and in every possible direction. And since these makers and keepers of chlorophyll — cyanobacteria, plankton and plants — are in charge of life on earth, it's only right that we begin with them, in particular with green plants, since they came about some 470 million years ago to enable the rest of us to live and breathe. That is quite a debt we owe them and we really ought not to behave like reckless, senseless hoodlums: hacking, burning, slashing and slaughtering them the way we are! Because, quite simply, if they go, we go.

CHAPTER 2:
EMERALDS FROM THE MUD

Many, many decades ago, when I was in school (I forget which grade), one of our 'General Science' topics was 'germination.' We had to take some black-eyed peas (rongi or lobia), or mustard seeds, or even grains of wheat, and place them on a wad of damp cotton wool. And we had to observe what happened over the next couple of days. Now anyone who has used a pea-shooter knows just how badly dried peas or, for that matter, black-eyed peas can sting you in the back of your neck when shot out of one. They were hard as pebbles, so I didn't expect much to happen. But hey presto — very soon, the black-eyed pea had softened and sprouted a pale root which went sprawling across the wad of damp cotton. And a shoot, encasing two tiny folded-up leaves in the seed, began uncoiling itself, the leaves slowly unfurling.

All too soon it was time to transplant this baby plant into a pot so it could get on a proper adult plant diet: sucking up what minerals and salts and nourishment it could glean from the soil, and the water I occasionally sprinkled on it. I kept it in the verandah and guarded it like a rottweiler from the ants that swarmed all over it. To my delight it grew and grew and then actually flowered, and then a pod appeared in which there were, guess what? More black-eyed peas! I was hugely elated and ever since have regarded seeds with a great deal of respect for the power they hold within their tiny bodies.

There was more astonishment in store. During one botany class, I think we were asked to split open a peanut and look closely at the two halves. At the top of one half were what looked like two tiny curled-up leaves, ready for their entry into the world. Though I am a hardcore carnivore I still feel a pang whenever I pop a peanut into my mouth, thinking about those two tiny leaves which would never see the light of day but instead the charnel house that was my tummy! And it made me think of all the tall stories we tell our children about not swallowing seeds: if you do, for example, swallow watermelon seeds, a watermelon might grow inside you, which would not be pleasant and – if you are a girl – make outraged adults believe that you've been naughty with your boyfriend! Actually many seeds, such as apple seeds, are bitter and poisonous to prevent animals from chomping them, usually they are covered with such a tough skin that they just pass through the gut, undamaged and not harming the creature that swallowed them.

Speck to Supergiant

But really, it is all about power! A seed the size of a pinhead has the potential to grow into something as grand and king-sized as a banyan tree — regarded as the 'kalpavriksh', the 'tree of life' and sentinel of the forest. Bacteria and viruses, which are not visible to the naked eye, have power far beyond what they ought to. Some of them put it to good use — like the good bacteria in our gut — others to sicken and kill us — like the evil Covid-19 virus!

These days, instant gratification (in conjunction with shortened attention spans) is the mantra. We want action — NOW! Most plants unfortunately seem to live life in extreme slow motion! That's what makes them (and botany) boring for so many of us. But thanks to time lapse photography, we can see plants live as they would if they lived by our hectic time scale. And boy, they can be as ruthless as a pack of painted wolves. Watch a 'tori' (zucchini) creeper send out feelers towards anything it can support itself on, usually a neighbouring plant, in time-lapse and you will be stunned. First it will swing around its tendrils, like a lasso, searching for a victim. Once it finds something it will twine itself around it several times, like a coil spring, as if garrotting it, and swarm higher and higher towards the sun, its leaves spreading out from the stalks like sails every which way. One summer, I was away for a month. When I left, the innocent tori creeper in one corner of my garden was crawling around in the grass, taking baby steps. When I got back it had completely engulfed a dwarf palm tree! A clothes rack kept close to it was annexed during the course of a single night! Here in Delhi, they are growing rapacious creepers like this near the notorious vilayati keekar (Acacia juliflora) that has colonized the Delhi Ridge near my home, hoping they will shroud the trees and so block out the sunlight, thus starving the invader of sunlight and killing the colonizer. But with some plants like the delicate 'touch-me-not' (mimosa) or 'chhui-mui' you can actually see the tiny leaflets fold up when they are touched: all hydraulics and ions at work! Some species of bamboo, which I like to think of as a form of Brobdingnag grass, may grow nearly 1 metre in a single day!

Peepul Power and King Kalpavriksh

The ambition of all plants, including these creepers, is to get as much sunlight as they possibly can, so they will search it out. Some, of course, have to go one step further: not only do they cling on to other plants but they send their roots into them to suck out the nutrients stored in the trunk and boughs. The mighty fig family (including our worshipped peepul and the kingly banyan) is notorious for this. A bird, say a hornbill, having dined happily on the figs, downloads the seeds on an innocent neem tree, let's assume. The seed, stuck on a branch, sniffs the air and immediately sends down a root towards the ground. Once it hits the ground it begins sending up nourishment, which in turn causes a shoot to, well, shoot up, heading for the heights and sunlight, sprouting leaves on the way so that the plant can open its own kitchen and make its own food. The first roots that hit the ground are strong and are called prop roots because that will be their ultimate function. But this is not enough — more roots swarm down from the shoot, girdling the trunk and sinking their tips into the cracks, sucking out nourishment. The poor 'host' neem is gradually squeezed and garrotted to death, starved of nourishment.

When I was first shown a strangler fig at the Corbett National Park, I was horrified. The tree itself resembled nothing but a scaffolding, standing tall without support. A hollow in the middle, like a chimney, was all that was left of the poor host tree, which had died a long time ago. The roots that the fig tree sends out are mighty powerful: if the seeds germinate on a building, the roots will split apart the brick and concrete, and they are stubbornly resistant to removal. That's why you never should plant a fig of any kind near your house. But yes, mighty as it might be, the banyan cannot afford to have an inflated ego, because its own survival is dependent on an insect that is virtually too small to see with the naked eye and who we will meet later in this book. Whenever I pass a gigantic banyan tree lording it over all it surveys, I keep thinking of the minuscule wasp that must have started it all, maybe over a hundred years ago. There's a lesson in this somewhere for all those who have become too big for their boots!

Vegans? Us? Bah!

Not all plants move in slow motion! Firstly, not all plants are vegans. The Venus flytrap, sundew and bladderwort are carnivores, using their sweet juices to lure, trap and suck dry gullible insects. In order to catch its victims, the Venus flytrap springs its barbed gin trap, also called snap trap, mousetrap or bear trap, in the blink of an eye. (Other plants may use more passive methods – a deviously slippery slope, for example, down which the insect slides into a hellhole full of digestive juices!) As most plants don't have muscles like ours, they use hydraulics – the pressure liquids can exert and the same principle that works in the brakes in your car, which is why you need brake fluid! That along with tiny amounts of electricity. And then there's attention to detail. The trap mechanism in the Venus flytrap has a time interval set for between 0.5 and 30 seconds: if there is a second disturbance within this time frame, it will snap shut. The snap itself takes less than a second, and the barbed leaves close tighter the more the insect struggles. Some plants increase the production of nectar if they sense bees or other pollinating insects humming around them, inviting them over for a meal!

As schoolkids we have all swiped at bushes and branches, ripping leaves off just for the heck of it. Well, that's not a very nice thing to do – especially since scientists are now telling us that leaves and plants (and trees) may actually scream (though not in our range of hearing) when being so treated! The knowledge makes me feel guilty every time I shave off a strip of curry patta leaves and drop them in hot oil: they go off like ladhis (string bombs), crackling and hissing!

It's certainly much more soothing and yogic to watch a leaf unfurl. Of course, there are myriad ways in which they do so, but typically, the newborn leaf will first be tightly curled up, pale yellow or white. Then, day by day it unfurls. Many newborn leaves — like that of the peepul — are a glossy red or scarlet at first and are heavily loaded with poison to prevent predation by herbivores. Then chlorophyll kicks in and they turn a fresh pale green — and they begin their life's work of making food for the tree.

Blistered Be Thy Tongue!

Fight or flee, those are the two options most living creatures have when some other living creature — or natural calamity — threatens to devour them. Plants unfortunately can't run away. Which is why it is so easy for us to hack them down: can you imagine if entire forests could either flee or rise up and charge to attack us, or if lianas could lasso us with their tendrils and strangle or hang us as we pass them by! (Frankly, deforesters deserve nothing less!) So, the only option left to them is to stand and fight!

This they do in various ways. Some plants (like cacti, roses and bougainvillea) modify some of their leaves into prickles and thorns. (I have two sisters, so I call myself the rose between two thorns!) Cacti are famous for their thorns, as are members of the acacia family, whose branches are fearsomely spiked, discouraging marauding goats and other livestock and herbivores. In Africa, however, the giraffes have got leather-tough tongues and lips and simply crunch them up anyway! The leaves of the stinging nettle, the bichchu booti so common in our hills, are barbed with poison-tipped hypodermics which discharge their venom when threatened. On the Delhi Ridge, I was once stuck fast in a thornbush for nearly half an hour, unable to break free, until I had painstakingly unhitched every hooked barb that had tagged my clothes and was trying to dig into my flesh and bleed me to death! (Now I knew what a fish might feel like when it was hooked! Not nice!)

Other plants stock up their leaves with poison, such as tannin. Tannin, which is also found in tea, and which is what makes it bitter, irritates the stomach's lining and discourages a second helping, especially among browsers and livestock. This is also why tea is so popular in the poorer countries of the world, because it kills the appetite. Leaves of grass are serrated with silica (basically glass), which does the same thing and is also why your sensible dog or cat will eat grass after it has illegally indulged in something like half a kilo of butter from the fridge: the silica irritates the stomach lining and makes the animal feel sick and puke out what it has just gobbled up.

Plants store their poisons in their leaves, stalks and stems, which are usually the main target of any marauder. A host of insects — ants, wasps, caterpillars — as well as mammals almost entirely dine off leaves, and here a full-frontal arms race goes on. Caterpillars know that poisons are usually concentrated around the midrib of the leaf and will carefully avoid this section while consuming it. Other insects — like those of the milkweed butterfly, the 'tigers' and monarchs — have evolved to absorb these poisons and use them for their own purposes: to make the butterflies unpalatable for birds. Some insects and caterpillars just snip off the stalk, letting the poison drip off, and then help themselves! It has been said that the deadly poison-arrow frogs of South and Central America absorb their deadly poison from the poisonous insects and creepy crawlies they consume, which in turn are locked and loaded with the poisons they have acquired from the plants they eat! Interesting menu choices these guys make!

Some of the poisons manufactured by plants can be very deadly indeed: the sap or 'milk' of the yellow oleander can, for instance, give a cow a cardiac arrest. We have used many of these poisons – like the alkaloids found in the lovely foxglove – to make drugs and sometimes to get rid of someone we detest. Other deadly plants (and seeds) include the notorious aak (calatropis) and the highly tempting 'rosary beads', which are a seductive red. More than 25 per cent of all drugs manufactured are plant-based, so their value just cannot be underestimated.

On a visit to the Yamuna Biodiversity Park in Wazirabad, North Delhi, I was being shown around their medicinal garden. 'Oh, that's good for the kidneys, this is good if you have diabetes, this is for heart conditions, and that for liver problems.' Every single plant there was pharmaceutical! It was like walking around a pharmacy – and many of these plants you would probably not even notice even as they grew all around you. Really, what I learned was that destroying plants can be injurious to your health! And alas, destroying plants (and trees) is what we're doing on a monumental scale, and impairing not only our own well-being but that of every living creature on the planet.

Not only does an individual plant or tree protect itself the best way it can but it also sounds the alarm among its kith and kin when a predator is around. When one tree or plant (like the tobacco plant, for example) is attacked it sends out warning pheromones to its neighbours, who immediately beef up their defences: more poison is produced and sent to the leaves, increasing their potency.

Birds Do It, Bees Do It, But Plants Get It Done

Like the genes of every living creature, those of plants are also eager to propagate themselves: The next gen is all they live for. As they can't move, and because there are no dating apps available to them, they have to resort to sneakier ways to make babies. They enlist other living creatures, mainly insects and mammals (bats and us) as matchmakers. Generally, every plant has a gentleman part (its pollen on the tip of its stamens, which is basically sperm) and a lady part (the stigma and ovary) where its unfertilized seeds live. Now it will usually not do (though it does happen) that the gentleman and lady parts of the same plant make babies together — we'd call that incest, they call it self-pollination! So, the pollen has to find the seeds of another plant in order to procreate. It enlists outside help; it must lure others to do this work for it (how demeaning this is, what a killjoy system!). So, it decks itself up in colourful petals (again, specialized leaves), spreads perfume in the air and lures in insects, birds and small mammals with sweet nectar (the old sweetheart scam all over again!) and its intoxicating, heavenly scent. The patterns on a petal, when seen in ultraviolet light, which is visible to insects, are often like runway lights, guiding the insect in with pinpoint accuracy. Again, attention to detail, detail, detail! Bees hum in, hummingbirds and sunbirds hover close, probing with their lance-like bills, all partaking of the sweet nectar. As if blessing them, the flower anoints its guests with pollen, on their foreheads, or fills up special pollen bags which bees carry on their legs (like food delivery boys carry gigantic knapsacks on their backs). Some plants like the heliconia are canny enough to ration the amount of nectar they make available to each visitor, so they ensure a wide spectrum of guests and wide pollen distribution. Bees and birds have to visit thousands of blooms if they are to be satiated. At another stop, they suck up more nectar and also deposit some of the pollen they have collected on the sticky stigma of the plant. The pollen is sent down a pollen tube and through it dispatches two sperms to the ovary. One of the sperms consummates the marriage with the waiting seed (hallelujah!) while the other turns into endosperm, which provides nourishment for the newborn seed. Ingenious!

Perfect Parenting

But these seeds have to get out of their pod prisons if they are to grow into independent plants themselves, and their parents have devised any number of astonishing and cunning ways by which they get rid of their offspring. (Parents, pay attention!) Some of these pod prisons can be as strong as a maximum-security cell or a bank safe when the seed is not ready to make its entrance into the big bad world outside, but this is only temporary.

Perhaps the friendliest and canniest way to send seeds off into the world is by bribery: by developing a sweet, juicy, fleshy fruit around the seed(s). Fruit is what the ovary turns into after fertilization

by the sperm: you know, mangoes, kiwis, papaya, pomegranate, chickoo, apples, oranges, bananas, et al. All greedily consumed by birds, insects, reptiles, amphibians, mammals and ourselves. Producing fruit takes time as the plant has to collect all the ingredients — like sugar, water and all the other flavouring and pulpy agents — and cook (ripen) them in the sun. Until such time that the plant is satisfied that the product has passed quality control and is ready for consumption, the fruit is protected by the skin or is horribly bitter or sour — ever tried to peel or eat a raw banana? The seed itself is often protected by a hard casing and, if consumed, either passes through the digestive tract of the consumer or is spat out, or is carefully set aside and planted. Some plants develop highly nutritious nuts and grains (endosperm) — which birds and squirrels and we consume or store away — some of which they and we forget where, others which just fall or are spilled by the wayside... enabling the plant to germinate.

I guess it all seems like rather extreme parenting! First the little seed is held prisoner in its case, then its parent covers it with sweet, delicious flesh, offering it as 'sacrifice' to anyone who would care to take a bite. But the tiny seed survives even this 'trial-by-intestine' and eventually sprouts!

Can You Make a Plum?

Just pause here to think about your favourite fruit. Let's say peaches or plums, or mangoes. You bite into one and sweet, flavourful juice spurts everywhere. The flesh is so soft and sweet you can only close your eyes in bliss. And every fruit has its own personal flavour. Which means it has its own special secret recipe for making it: so much sugar, so much water, so much natural flavouring to be added, so much this and that for pulp and body, slow cook in the sun for so many days or weeks, make sure the colour is right and so on. Of course, we're trying desperately to synthesize fruit juice but mostly end up just squeezing the fruit and canning or tetra-packing the juice, and in an unintended admission of its superiority swear that 'no artificial flavours were added', except, umm, some sugar and preservatives. So far there's no way we can manufacture an artificial apple in a factory! Or for that matter a single apple seed. That is why seeds are so invaluable and need to be preserved at all costs. We may help the seed to grow by planting it in rich soil and watering it and fussing over it, but we can't make it, whether at home or in the most advanced, sophisticated laboratory or factory in the world. That is something we ought never to forget.

Travelling Far

Plants also get rid of their seeds by air, overland and by sea. In some plants (the Himalayan balsam, for example) the pressure inside the seed pod increases due to evaporation and it explodes, scattering the seeds as far as possible from the parent plant: the equivalent of lazy-bum adult children being given a boot in the pants and being told to go out and earn their keep! In other cases, like in the silk cotton tree and dandelion, for example, the seed is swathed in light silky fibres, and when the pod bursts the seeds parachute far, far away. Some seeds are attached to wings and propellers and just flutter away: the membranous wings of some tropical lianas are so aerodynamically perfect that our wind-tunnel whiz kids are still trying to figure out how to copy them for use in airplane wings. Every child ought to have blown on a dandelion and watched the result with wonder and delight. Walk through a field of grass, shrub or savannah, and you (and your dog) will have burrs containing seeds armed with grappling iron hooks, or which are just plain sticky, Velcroed all over on your clothes, skin or fur. You 'deseed' yourself and your pet and maybe the seed finds a new home from where to germinate. Coconut trees lean over the tideline, hoping to drop their nuts into the sea so that the tides can bear them away to distant coastlines and beaches. Some plants just depend on the wind and breeze to send their seeds off into the world. It doesn't do to drop seeds right next to the parent plant, because the latter does not share — neither nutrients, nor water nor sunlight, not even with its own babies.

Another astonishing facet of fruit is its packaging. We embalm everything in industrial strength plastic, and 'unboxing' has become a YouTube phenomenon in itself. But ever noticed how easy it is to peel a banana that is ripe? Or an orange for that matter. And we don't need to peel plums because they are just juice bombs!

Plants and trees unfortunately can't run away from us and so have fallen victim en masse to our predations. We've been levelling our rainforests at a frightening rate, without for a moment pausing to think that hey, we still can't manufacture a tree in a factory! We can plant a seed or put in a sapling or graft a twig, which will grow into a tree or bush eventually, but there is no factory like a car manufacturing plant that can produce a readymade tree to order. We can't even make a plank of wood!

The Wood Wide Web

It's now being found that plants and trees actually communicate with one another and even exchange nutrients via what's being called the wood wide web. Roots, which anchor the plant firmly to the earth, snuffle out and suck up moisture and nutrients from deep underground, spread far and wide, and are a vital part of the plant's communication and intelligence network. Root hairs cultivate fungi in a symbiotic (you scratch my back, I'll scratch yours) relationship that is called mycorrhizae. The fungi spread their mass of fine tentacles far and wide, much beyond the reach of the roots, supplying water and nutrients such as phosphorous back to the roots and tree. They even link up with other fungi tentacles sent hither by other trees in the locality and make barter deals with them, exchanging news, nutrients and warnings! Of course, there's no such thing as a free lunch, and so the fungi tax the tree 30 per cent of its sugar production for their own use.

We Should Be Hung, Drawn and Quartered

What's astonishing and shameful is how dispensable we think trees are. And how, without ever being able to move an inch, trees always seem to come in our way. So, if we want a broader road, because there are just too many cars running amuck, we hack down the trees that might be shading that road. In winter we complain that it's too cold because of the trees shading our houses and hack off huge boughs and then complain in summer that it's too hot! We're even cutting swathes through protected areas, sanctuaries and national parks, to build our expressways. Massive forests have been felled for building colossal dams which don't really work in the long run and just clog up rivers and constipate entire ecosystems, not to mention the livelihoods of those dependent on and living in those areas. During the Vietnam war, the Americans defoliated 31,000 square kilometres of Vietnamese rainforest with their lovely concoction Agent Orange – the dreadful effects of which are still being felt by millions (it's been called ecocide). They still lost the war. 'Development' projects sprout up everywhere, and forests are cleared for glittery resorts and hotels. Drive along the borders of the Corbett National Park and the experience is nothing short of schizophrenic. On one side of the road are rows of glitzy resorts and hotels, blazing with lights and belting out cacophonic music from jumbo speakers; on the other the silent, brooding forest. Palm oil plantations in Indonesia have rendered the wonderful orangutan nearly homeless and facing a very bleak future indeed. And our government is now casting a covetous eye at the lush rainforests of the North East, replete with endemic species, for this purpose – more on this in later chapters.

Oh yes, we say suavely, for every tree we cut we'll plant ten, or hundred, saplings. Where we would do this is one question, and how we would look after the saplings is another. Transplanting trees has become the buzzword these days, but the survival rate of such trees is abysmal. I would suggest that before we hack down a tree, we should plant those ten or hundred saplings and wait for them to reach the same age and size as that of the tree/s we want to bring down. That will show commitment! Oh, we say, satellites show that the areas under green cover are increasing in the country. That's because we're now counting sterile lawns and golf courses and back gardens and playing fields as 'green areas'. What next? Astroturf and tennis hardcourts painted green will be called green areas too? Healthy forest ecosystems, which is what we need to stave off global warming and climate change, are reducing radically.

We try to console ourselves by saying that trees don't feel any pain while being hacked bit by bit. That too is now under scrutiny and it's going to be a terrible day when the opposite is proved beyond all doubt, and we can hear playbacks of trees and plants screaming as an axe plunges into them, or a power saw slices through them. The high-pitched scream of a power saw is probably one of the most hideous sounds in the world.

What a Tree Does

Let's just think again of a little seed's achievement. From being something the size of a pinhead, it has, by using nothing but water, air, sunlight and a few minerals it can glean from the mud, grown in complete silence and causing no pollution, into something that may tower over 100 meters into the sky. At the same time, it plays host to a bewildering variety of other life forms — algae, fungi, insects, birds, reptiles and mammals — who may use it for sustenance, residence, to climb up on or simply to lie under on a hot summer day. All the while pumping out oxygen and sucking in carbon dioxide and storing it in the form of carbon. Sure, it takes its time to grow, but then plants always believed in the slow and steady. Maybe it's time we did too.

So many of us who live in teeming, choking cities, 'concrete jungles' like Mumbai, Delhi, Kolkata and Bengaluru, frequently go driving off to hill stations, national parks and anywhere there are forests and trees. In our cities we (and our dogs) go for walks and jogs in parks and gardens. Even in our concrete pillbox homes, we festoon our verandahs with indoor plants and window boxes and if we're lucky enough to have a garden, well, that's where we go to when the boss has been a prat. No matter how synthetic a life we may live, we really can't do without greenery, literally and figuratively.

As for global warming and trees, here's a very local and literal example of what trees do: Back in the 1990s, I often had to drive down a broad open road (the Ring Road) on the way home in the height of a Delhi summer, when the temperature regularly stayed above 40 degrees Celsius. At that time my car was not air-conditioned, and even the car felt the heat, with the temperature gauge often nudging the red line and the engine pinking. I could feel the heat radiate off my face, and my eyes smarted. The breeze itself felt like it was fresh off a furnace. The moment I turned into the side road that led to my house, and which abutted a very shady park, I felt as if I had suddenly entered an air-conditioned space, and the car's temperature gauge swung back into the green section, making the car sound happier!

Rainforests make their own weather and rain. As the trees exhale vast amounts of water vapor every day, this rises in the heat and by late afternoon accumulates in the form of great roiling thunderheads, which let go of their contents over the canopy. This is why they are called rainforests.

This is also why, even as we enjoy our sarso ka saag or broccoli souffle, and especially as we are being increasingly urged towards a plant-based diet, we must treat all plants and trees with the respect and TLC they deserve. They look after our mind and body and spiritual well-being. And we must never forget that mighty indispensable emerald molecule at their heart: chlorophyll.

CHAPTER 3:
THE TINY TITANS
THAT RULE THE WORLD

Butterflies in Party Frocks

For a long time, my attitude towards most everyday insects and other creepy-crawlies was simple: flies and mosquitoes had to be swatted, cockroaches flattened with a rolled-up newspaper, bees and wasps avoided. Butterflies were silly dilettantes who indulged in drunken flying, moths were morons, hellbent on kamikaze flights into bright lights and spiders' webs could trigger momentary panic as you blundered into them. You were wary of red ants but black ants were okay and could be flicked off your sandwich easily. It gave me immense pleasure to pick ticks off my dogs, drop them into a can of kerosene and watch them sink to the bottom. And yes, to tap a grasshopper's bottom and watch it zing away.

I'm not sure when this attitude began to change but then one day, waiting for someone to answer the doorbell, I idly glanced at the kumquat (Chinese orange) plant in the portico. What looked like a tiny bird dropping caught my eye: the doing of some small bird, I thought, grinning. Then my eyebrows shot up, because the 'bird dropping' moved. I peered closely, and realized that it was a caterpillar, munching away at the leaf. Of course, I knew that caterpillars eventually turned into chrysalises, which in turn became butterflies. Well, I thought, why not see how exactly this happened. I searched the plant and found perhaps two more caterpillars chomping away, as well as tiny pearl white eggs adhering to the leaves. I put the caterpillars in a time-honoured jam jar along with a plentiful supply of kumquat leaves and twigs, which I replaced every day. I knew that in spite of being wholesale gluttons, caterpillars were notoriously fussy about their diet: these ones would only feed on the leaves of the kumquat or other citrus plants and certainly refuse a bunch of fresh palak (spinach), which surely should be so good for them.

Certainly, they were gluttons. They chomped and chomped, and seemed to be late diners, eating through the night rather than during the day, when they pretended to be bird shit! Really this was a stroke of genius: caterpillars are many a bird's favourite dish, something on which most baby birds are nourished (soft, juicy, oozy, you get the drift!). But which self-respecting bird would eat its own potty or worse feed it to its babies? Well, caterpillar grew and grew and one morning I found it had changed into a handsome green, now exactly matching the colour of the leaves that it decimated. During the day it would lie along the midrib of the leaf, virtually invisible, then pig it out through the night (nice overnighters, eh?). Its own potty, which is called frass, was shot out as far away from it as possible, so predators wouldn't cotton on to its presence. It ate ravenously, sawing along the edges

45

of the leaves, its jaws rasping. If you blew on it, it would rear up, extending two horn like orange protuberances from its head, pretending to be a snake!

All this bingeing naturally meant that it put on weight. So, it had to upsize from time to time. The now tight old skin would split and shed and hey presto, beneath it a new soft, pliable outfit would be in place. This happened several times and eventually, the caterpillar decided to atone for its gastronomic sins and go on a fast. Not only that, from its mouth it extruded silken strands and fashioned a hammock: the chrysalis (or pupae), from which it slung itself on one of the twigs. Now it went into a state of deep meditation. And check out the astonishing attention to detail: my first lot of caterpillars was raised during the monsoons, and the chrysalis were leaf green, whereas those that I raised post-monsoon were twig brown because now that was the fashionable shade.

After a week or so of meditation along with occasional twitches, the chrysalis appeared to be darkening and drying out and then, one evening I could see the butterfly inside it, speckled in black and pale yellow, rolled up like a Brit's brolly. I knew it was getting ready to emerge, so set the alarm for 4 o'clock the next morning. It made me wait for two hours, twitching and bucking from time to time. And then, it split the husk of its pupa and emerged tiredly, somewhat like an astronaut climbing out of a space capsule. Its wings were crumpled as crepe paper, and it crawled tiredly onto a twig and hung them down to dry. Blood pumped through the veins in its wings, stretching them out and then stiffening them, essential if the insect was to fly.

Newly minted,
it was perfect!
Its eyes were
large   and
lustrous,   black
as obsidian, the
proboscis curled up
like a watch spring,
the filamentous legs
felt around tentatively,
the wings were speckled
and with smudges of orange and
mauve. It was a brand-new lime butterfly, quite common, but
no less beautiful for it. After about fifteen minutes it finally flew
off; it would now suck up nectar and search for a partner — its
chief goal in life. Wow, I thought, what a lifestyle: to be an out
and out glutton and then a fasting, meditating hermit, and then
to turn into something so delicate, dressed up in a party frock,
sipping nectar. Cinderella, take that!! But how the heck did this
astonishing metamorphosis happen?

That answer was something as devious as anything Mother
Nature could conjure up! When a caterpillar hatches it has two
sets of cells. One, the caterpillar cells, and two, 'secret' cells
containing the blueprint for the butterfly it will eventually become.
As it eats, the caterpillar cells grow bigger and bigger — they do
not, like most cells, subdivide. Hormones ensure that the potential
butterfly cells remain dormant. Eventually when the caterpillar is
fat enough, hormones again switch off the caterpillar's 'go binge'
command and order the cells to self-destruct, and the hormones

stifling the butterfly cells give the go-ahead signal for them to develop. The caterpillar cells now dissolve into a rich soup or smoothie on which the growing butterfly cells nourish themselves and develop into various parts of the butterfly.

Of course, we've also discovered that if we boil the silken cocoon of the silkworm moth we can unravel the silken threads and produce, well, silk: that wonderful material prized all over the world and now a part of a multi-billion-dollar industry. But we can't produce a single strand of silk ourselves.

Incidentally, butterflies do not only sip nectar like wine-sipping socialites at a diplomatic soirée: they appreciate blood, sweat, tears (sometimes yours), dung, rotting meat and mud for all the salts and minerals they contain. And they are tough: they can tolerate sudden changes in atmospheric pressure that would bring down an elephant, and some migrate thousands of kilometres – the monarch of North America and Canada is one classic example. As winter draws in the monarchs living in the northern parts of the United States and in Canada begin an epic 4,500-kilometre flight to a relatively tiny patch of forest in Mexico, where millions congregate over winter. As spring and summer come around, they flex their wings and take off, heading back north. But get this: the journey back up north is done by three to five generations of butterflies which are hatched en route, as if participating in a relay. The generation that flew down south mate, lay eggs and die as the season changes, and their progeny then fly a few hundred kilometres north at a time. During the course of their journey, they too mate and die, and their progeny continues the northwards journey. How exactly the various generations of butterflies navigate is a mystery.

When Dragons Emerge from the Deep

And this is just one of the myriad mind-boggling stunts and seeming miracles insects can pull off. Dragonflies have around 30,000 lenses in each eye: imagine if they had to be fitted with contact lenses! They were the first insect hunters to fly, and evolved 300 million years ago, with wingspans of up to 70 centimetres. They are much smaller now, apparently thanks to reducing levels of oxygen over the millennia (and thank God for us!), but remain voracious hunters, even cannibalizing their own kind. Their legs, hopeless for walking, evolved into barbed wire baskets in which they scoop up their prey on the wing and chomp them up in flight. They can beat each of their four cellophane-like wings, often so beautifully stained, independently. Like most flying insects their wings can twist and turn about their axis while flapping, thus enabling them to generate lift both on the upstroke and downstroke by creating little tornadoes of air off the edges of their wings (among birds, only the hummingbird is capable of this). They are fiercely territorial, patrolling air corridors where they hunt and will charge you (I have been charged several times) if you intrude into their airspace.

Now for the googly! Most of the dragonflies' lives — perhaps two or three years — are actually spent underwater, in ponds and streams! The 'naiads' or 'nymphs' that hatch from the eggs — laid beneath the water — are anything but. They are frightful creatures, armed with a switchblade-like jaw which flashes out in the blink of an eye, plunging into and drawing back its terrorized victims into its mouth — small fish, tadpoles and the like. Eventually they crawl out of the water up a stalk and here change their attire, emerging as pale etiolated dragonflies. In a short while, they are ready for aerial combat! They can top out at around 78 kmph, and the segments in their body are so arranged as to absorb the shock of impact when they wham into their victims at this speed.

Honeymoon Hunter

One of my all-time favourite insects is the praying mantis. Tall and twiggy as an embittered spinster headmistress, she is a chinless assassin, equipped with enormous bead-like eyes which can see in 3D. She attains a posture of hypocritical worship, barbed legs thrust out beseechingly as if in supplication. Let a bee or a fly whiz past, and the legs flash out and embrace the victim like a gin-trap snapping, and the head comes down and the chomping begins – rather in the manner of someone eating a bhutta. She may be emerald, rose, or caramel, often camouflaged to match the foliage or flowers she perches on.

Her dark notoriety stems from the fact that she munches on her husband – during their honeymoon itself. Talk about love bites! Some say she rips off his head, lunching on his brains, while other reports maintain that she may bite him clean in half. Whatever the case, the poor guy's nether end continues doing its duty, making the mantis perhaps the only creature to have a headless lover! It's also believed that the nerves in the groom's nether end are disconnected from his brain (this is a no-brainer really), so it keeps doing what it has been programmed to do: getting the lady pregnant! Recent reports, however, have somewhat salvaged her reputation as apparently most lady mantises in the wild don't dine off their beloveds during the honeymoon, as the tabloids would prefer. In the lab, while being ogled at by voyeuristic scientists, they come under considerable pressure... and make their husbands lose their heads!

Cocks of the Rock: Roaches

Cockroaches of course are not everyone's cup of tea (though I suspect I once inadvertently imbibed tiny cockroach babies, mistaking them for coffee powder on the rim of the mug, which made my niece gleefully announce that I had just had 'Coffee Cockaroachee!'). Usually, cockroaches prefer it when and where it's dark and they're able to squeeze into tiny cracks. They are real toughies, and once we have annihilated every living creature on the earth in a nuclear holocaust, they will probably be the only survivors to crawl out of the devastation and wave their feelers around, ready to get on with their lives. They eat decaying organic material (plants, animals) and their poop releases nitrogen into the soil, which is vital for the growth of forests. And they can live headless for a week, which would have given the French revolutionaries something to think about!

51

Billions of Blistering Beetles!

The beetle clan, which is the biggest, with over 400,000 described species (and many more awaiting their Aadhaar cards), have many stars: my personal favourite has to be dung beetles, trundling across the ground or flying en masse once they get the scent of an oh-so-dreamy, steamy, creamy potty in the air. Some couples pick off bits of dung, roll them into perfectly round balls and hustle these off towards holes in the earth where they live, pushing them back with their hind legs. Usually, the gentleman does the heavy lifting while the lady assists by seemingly yelling directions. If disoriented, the gentleman will climb aboard the ball, circle around and reorient himself with the help of the sun's position. They are even known to use starlight, the Milky Way no less, for this purpose! Once they've got the dungball safely inside their home, they may dine on it and the lady lays her eggs on it, so that the grub has nourishment readily available. As recyclers of waste, dung beetles are invaluable: when settlers landed in Australia with their vast flocks and herds of sheep and cattle, the local dung beetles turned up their noses at this imported dung. (They only liked kangaroo doo-doo.) To prevent Australia going knee-deep in dung — causing disease-spreading blowflies to go berserk — they had to import dung beetles from other parts of the world to do the needful! This was one case where the introduction of an alien species worked (unlike Australia's disaster with cane toads). Dung beetles are invaluable in that they process stinking, bacteria-infected dung and turn it into rich, nutritious soil.

Fireflies, also called glowworms or lightning bugs, are neither flies nor worms nor bugs, but beetles. On misty monsoon evenings in the mountains, there is perhaps nothing as blissful as to stand hand-in-hand with your sweetheart, watching these ethereal beetles waft through the pines, winking their frosty green lights at one another. This luminescence is caused by two chemicals, luciferase and the enzyme luciferin, reacting together with the help of oxygen, phosphorous and a power bank called adenosine triphosphate, all three of which all of us have and which power our muscles. Every species of firefly has its own special flashing frequency so that they meet and match with their own kind. It's the gents that flash their 'are you available tonight' queries as they float through the trees, and the ladies, waiting on the foliage beneath, that reciprocate with their decision. There is one species of firefly named Photuris where the lady flashes her signal, not to a gentleman of her own species, but to that of another species called Photinus. The poor misguided fool approaches her, full of expectation — until the femme fatale strikes! She pounces and devours him.

Oh Honey!

We can't live without bees and are stupidly annihilating them big time all over the world. One third of all the food we consume is pollinated by insects and mammals, but mainly honeybees, which not only do this for us, but also produce delicious honey from the nectar the plants bribe them with. By habitat destruction, deforestation and the spraying of pesticides like Schwarzenegger blazing forth with an AK 47, we have decimated bee populations around the world. Beekeeping has become a big business, and beekeepers now travel hundreds of miles with their hives in order to pollinate fields that otherwise would remain barren. Of course, we had to be greedy, so we tried cross-breeding ferocious African bees with the more tolerant European species, in the hope of getting increased yields of honey. That didn't happen and instead, we ended up with monstrous Africanized bees, which escaped from the labs they were bred in, and which now are rapidly colonizing and terrorizing the United States. A lesson here for all those tinkering with genetic engineering!

Honeybees of course are known for their famous 'waggle dance' – a wriggling, writhing manoeuvre that worker bees perform on returning from nectar-scouting sorties. The dance, rather like instructions given by Google maps, indicates the distance, direction, quantity and quality of the nectar source so other bees can make a beeline for it. More recent research has indicated that bees might indeed also be sentient and that the larvae of potential queens, waiting to emerge from their cells, actually 'quack', urging their sisters in the hive to release them. When one is released, she runs around 'tooting' and massacring all the other potential queen larvae that haven't been so quick on the draw. Whatever next! You can actually watch YouTube videos about this.

As every child is aware, bees (like the infamous rock bees of India) can sting: they do this in defence of their hives, but unfortunately, rip out their own innards in the process, ensuring their own deaths. So, insects too can be martyrs. Just be aware: if you are allergic to bee stings, stay away from them and if stung get to a hospital ASAP! And once a bee stings you, beat it, for it will have given the call to arms to the others in the hive and you certainly do not want to be swarmed. What I am still trying to figure out is what survival sense this makes. If the bee dies while stinging you, there's one soldier less to defend the hive. If, like wasps, they did not leave their stingers and intestines embedded in your flesh, they could live to sting another day. Go figure!

How Wicked Is That?

Wasps are not the most congenial of insects; with their slanting eyes and wire-thin waists, vivid striping and deadly stings they scream 'alien danger'. A bee can sting you but only once, a wasp as many times as it wants to. Many however are more interested in stinging their prey: spiders, cockroaches, bees, caterpillars and beetles, among others. This is when they turn truly diabolical: a lady wasp – like the extraordinarily beautiful jewel cockroach wasp of Africa and South Asia – will even dare take on a cockroach much bigger and tougher than herself. She'll first sting it on its front legs, paralyzing them and making the roach defenceless. Then she'll sting it in the head with a different venom, which goes straight to the brain and turns it into a docile zombie and her obedient servant. Thus anaesthetized, she drags it to a hole in the ground she has kept ready and stuffs it inside. The hole she later covers with detritus – dead leaves and grass. On the stupefied roach she now lays a precious egg. The ghastly grub that hatches now begins dining on the soft parts of the cockroach and then burrows in deep. But get this: very carefully it bypasses all the vital organs of the cockroach, such as the heart and circulatory system, in order to keep the insect alive as it dines off it so that the meat remains fresh! I once (in the interest of science) opened up the sealed home of a spider wasp in my room, that does much the same thing, and was horrified to discover the feebly moving bodies of eight or nine tiny spiders, on one of which this awful yellow grub had clamped itself. But think of all the hi-tech chemical engineering that must have gone into the manufacture of that anaesthetizing venom. It had to be powerful enough just to zombify the victim – not kill it. Ask a wildlife vet how difficult it is to calculate the right amount of anaesthetic needed to put an elephant down, but not kill it, nor cause it to awaken just as you are taking a blood sample from its ear!

Totalitarian Terrors

Ants are just everywhere and are perhaps best known for their totalitarian regimes. Colonies live and die for their queen. They go to war with each other, take prisoners and make them slaves, cut devastating swathes through rainforests in their pursuit of food and may even be farmers, harvesting leaves which they feed to fungi on which they and their larvae feed. They have, like so many other insects, divided their societies into 'castes'. Soldiers – which may also be blind – guard and fight for the colony, workers (all ladies and sisters of the queen, who has rendered them disinterested in sex by spreading a special 'no sex I'm a worker!' pheromone) do the housekeeping, feed and tend to the larvae and go scouting for food. The especially talented members look after and fuss over the queen who, bloated beyond belief, simply lies back and lays eggs by the thousand drones, the gentlemen, who just hang around doing nothing until it is time to fly and honeymoon with the queen when she needs to start a new colony.

Again, there is attention to detail. The entrance to the colony is guarded by what I call immigration and passport control. I've watched an ant returning to its colony being given the ant-equivalent of a pat-down and having its papers checked! One that didn't make the grade was attacked and sent packing. There are always infiltrators which may try to sneak in and eventually take over the colony by assassinating the queen or decimating the larvae.

But there are other dangers related to being a part of such a totalitarian regime and being so utterly brainwashed, which we will be wise to take note of: when scouts leave the colony they leave a scent trail, indicating to others the route they've taken and which helps them get back to the colony once they find something. Army ants (which are blind) use this to follow each other when on their marches. But if they backtrack onto their own trail, they end up in what's been called an ant-mill and will follow the trail in circles — until they literally drop dead. I once watched a big black ant do a similar thing in my bathroom around the rim of my soap dish. I had to rescue it before it dropped dead! That's why we need to fear totalitarian regimes and artificial intelligence too — they can make morons out of us and make us obey their every lunatic command blindly! There was a report in 2023 of a Belgian man who took his own life after listening, over a period of six weeks, to what an AI chatbot called Eliza had to say to him about global warming and the climate crisis. This Eliza for sure didn't wipe any tear from anyone's eye!

Like us, ants too seem to be in a terrible hurry to get around, but unlike us they do not crash headlong into each other. They will meet, exchange news and then scurry on their way. Their sense of smell is said to be five to six times better than that of dogs, and I've noticed this too. Removing a dead big black ant from the swimming pool, I placed it outside.
There was not a living creature in sight.
A couple of minutes later I
returned to see
if somehow the
'rescued' ant

had recovered and hey presto, it seemed as if it had: it was moving. Closer examination revealed it was being dragged by a tiny-tot ant rather in the manner of a tow truck pulling a 747. Then another ant came scurrying up and within minutes a whole column of them had poured out of the entrance to their colony and had got to work hauling the dead ant in. They seemed to be running helter-skelter every which way, shouting at one another, but they knew exactly what they were doing as they headed home. Getting the dead ant inside the colony (under an overhanging plinth at the corner of the pool) was a dicey operation, because the huge corpse had to be dangled mid-air over the pool, being held on to by those at the edge and then being hauled in by those waiting at the entrance. They did it with elan, and this was just the first helping they got that day as I retrieved other dead insects from the water to watch the whole process again and again. They had the mother of all buffets that morning! So, the next time you are in Chandni Chowk or Sadar Bazaar and are overwhelmed by the apparent chaos and crowds, take hope: there may be a method in this madness!

Radar Beetles

On the surface of ponds and streams you might have noticed little beetles pirouetting rapidly and whizzing every which way. These guys are whirligig beetles and they use 'radar' to latch on to their prey. By spinning around in circles as many as twelve times a second, they send out circular ripples which spread out from them. If there is a dead creature – say a drowned bee – in the water, the ripples will hit it and bounce back to the beetle, like radar waves do, indicating the position. And off the beetle zips for its meal, usually accompanied by others who have done exactly the same thing!

Come into My Parlour

Spiders are usually not a girl's best friend, not ever since Ms Muffet sat on her tuffet! Many are hairy (and can be as large as a dinner plate and can take down small birds), some are venomous and ferocious and they can be cunning beyond belief! They may set silken traps, or simply hunt by ambushing. Their USP of course has to be their ability to produce silk and weave webs. Several different kinds of silk, for several different purposes. Tough silk (stronger than steel wire of a similar diameter) for the scaffolding of their webs, which may stretch several meters across; strong, elastic silk, beaded with glue, to entrap their victims; presumably soft silk for their egg cases and anchoring silk as safety lines when they take leaps of faith! And gossamer for parasailing when they are babies leaving home!

If you have the patience, do watch an orb-weaving spider weave her web, a task usually embarked upon in the evening. It might take her half an hour but it will be well worth your time. Once done, the spider will sit in the middle of the web and wait. One morning on the Delhi Ridge, I watched, amazed, as eleven silly butterflies blundered into a web, driving the poor spider into a tizzy as she rushed from one to the other, trussing them up with silk for later use. She could have thrown a party that morning! Or at least entertained her husband. Some large orb webs, belonging to the Argiope family, for example, have a jagged white silken X radiating from the centre. We're still not sure of its purpose.

Some say it serves as a warning to birds. But if they do fly into the web, it's likely they will shred it.

Ah, and here is something about spiders that most girls will indeed applaud. Most lady spiders are several times the size and weight of their husbands, and these puny little guys have their work cut out if they want a piece of the action. If they disturb madam, she will rush out and devour them. So, seduction is the name of the game. Some hairy gents bring their lady-loves a silk-wrapped gift, like a cockroach (one cheapskate cheater even brings her gift-wrapped leaves, which she cannot eat!). While she is unwrapping her gift, he rushes in, does his thing and beats it. Others twang the strings of the web as if playing on a harp, hoping to lull the lady into a trance. Even so, in most cases he becomes the date and the dinner as she devours him regardless. It's a sacrifice not in vain, for his protein will serve their babies well.

Some spiders dig holes in the ground and fashion a silken trapdoor at the entrance, which snaps open the moment an insect stumbles over the traplines set outside. The spider then leaps out and grabs the startled victim in a trice. The diving bell spider builds a silken dome just underwater and takes and renews its own oxygen supply: it strokes off the bubbles of air adhering to its hirsute body when it slips underwater, creating a large bubble, which is its air supply. Oxygen is renewed by underwater foliage and fresh bubbles brought down from the top.

Spiders are prodigious consumers of insects (and others of their kind) and are invaluable in keeping pests in check.
So again, respect!

We of course are desperately trying to synthesize spider silk for our own nefarious (and not-so-nefarious) purposes. We're looking at bulletproof jackets, gunsights, sutures, seatbelts and the like. I read somewhere (and still can't believe it) that a web, with silk threads thick as a pencil, would be able to stop a Boeing 747 in mid-flight! Think of the uses something like that can be put to.

Weapon of Mass Destruction

Mosquitoes have killed more people than humans have managed to do in all of history (7 million a year), so it's no doubt that many of us think that the world would be a better place without them. Well, eradicating them is not proving easy — they just develop immunity to whatever toxic concoction we spray on them, and come back stronger. So, we're now trying to render them incapable of playing host to the deadly malarial parasite that they carry and pass on to us. But even mosquitoes have their uses: they've kept us away from prime tropical rainforests which we would have by now decimated for sure had they not been buzzing around.

High Flying Sickos

Flies of all kinds don't rank high in the popularity stakes: sure, they clean their feet diligently before they feed, but then they vomit all over their food before slurping it up, which is disgusting and not a habit you would like to encourage in your children. Like many arthropods they cannot digest solids so have to make smoothies of their food before slurping it up.

We can learn a thing or two about flying by observing flies do their double somersaults and upside-down landings on the roof. Their maggots have been used to clean up gangrenous wounds because they eat only dead tissue – something that was noticed by nurses in godforsaken battlefields, where wounded soldiers who were infested with maggots were not in as bad a condition as they ought to have been: the grubs had 'cleaned' and even disinfected their wounds, leaving only healthy living tissue behind.

Fruit flies, with whom we share many genes, have been used by scientists for an enormous range of experiments. Back in 1946 they were the first sentient living creatures to be sent into space and have even had babies there.

Tickle My Bum!

Grasshoppers, whose bums are such great fun to tickle, have an ingenious ratchet-kind of musculature which enables them to slowly store up energy in their thunder thighs before releasing it all at once, rather like you drawing back a catapult sling and then letting go. But they also have a very destructive avatar in the form of locusts. When the going is good, groups of grasshoppers conspire together, get madly friendly with each other and turn into great swarms of locusts, some hopping over the ground in great battalions, others darkening the skies with their numbers, demolishing everything in their path, to the extent of causing famines in countries! When nature goes berserk, she does so on a magnum scale.

How to Run the World

Around 90 per cent of all animal life consist of insects, 10 per cent of which feed off one another. One million species have been ticked off, with possibly 6 to 8 million awaiting to be recognized. Without them the earth would not be able to function. They clean up organic dead matter and keep their own populations and that of other creatures in check, they invigorate and aerate the soil, pollinate big time, ensuring that we do not run out of oxygen-producing plant life and the basis of all we eat. We have of course labelled many of them as pests because they interfere with our food production systems. This however is usually the first sign that something is out of balance and if anyone has upset nature's equilibrium, it has to be us. We have sprayed (and are continuing to spray) toxic chemicals in an irresponsibly reckless manner to be rid of them, killing the good, the bad and the ugly in the process and affecting nearly every form of life dependent on them, as these toxic concoctions enter the food chain. The classic example was pointed out by Rachel Carson back in the 1960s in her classic book *Silent Spring* (Houghton Mifflin, 1962): DDT caused the near extinction of the peregrine falcon (and other raptors), whose eggs were too fragile and thin-walled as a result of the parents' eating birds and insects that had ingested the pesticide in their diet. We've tried all sorts of insecticides to be rid of mosquitoes and they have only come back with stronger immunity in an arms race that we haven't yet won.

Ferocious hunters though they may be, these tiny-tot titans are also a vital food source for myriad creatures, including each other. Also for amphibians like frogs and toads, reptiles like lizards of all kinds, birds (which are big-time consumers) and especially hatchlings, even fish, mammals like ant-eaters and chimpanzees – and now us. Gram for gram they contain more protein than all traditional meats and fish – and we are now seriously considering including them into our diet in a major way. (Crispy-fried crickets and scrunchy, grilled dragonflies with soya sauce doesn't sound too bad, does it?)

So, the next time you see an ant trundle across the floor do not step on it. Give way and let it pass. As for that spider waiting in its web in the corner of the room: let it be, it's keeping the pesky mosquitoes, cockroaches and flies in check!

These tiny titans, true Atlases of the earth, are just a part of the massive maintenance crew looking after life on our potpourri planet. Now we'll meet a few more which are also extraordinarily talented, even though they may not be the most beloved: amphibians and reptiles.

CHAPTER 4: THE SLITHERY, SLICK AND SENSATIONAL

The Fab Froggies!

When has a frog not put a smile on your face? Oh, yes, sure there was that time in biology class when you were meant to dissect one with a surgeon's scalpel and were promptly sick and decided not to take up biology after all. Thankfully, live dissections are no longer needed; virtual ones are good enough. But yes, when a frog looks at you out of its big bulbous eyes, glimmering with emotion, and smiles – and it comes naturally to them – you can't help but smile back! Apart from smiling they can sing in chorus too! After a romantic monsoon downpour at dusk, a resounding chorus of 'berrek-berrek-berrek' breaks out from inundated fields and water bodies, turning on and off miraculously and making you squeeze your sweetheart's hand just a little harder. I once attended a rock concert by a band of some 200–300 bright yellow bullfrogs (with enormous blue cheek pouches) on the Delhi Ridge and it was like the Woodstock Fair!

Well, maybe not so much for the girls who were being jumped on by these hulks en masse and who kicked out like stallions at each other. And who can forget Mr Toad of Toad Hall in *The Wind in the Willows*? Incidentally, toads are actually just warty frogs.

But yes, you meet a little green frog in the swimming pool and your day just gets better. See, you do the breaststroke just the way it does it, but it learned it much before you did! But there's a lot more to frogs than just making you smile and showing you how to swim. Frogs make up 88 per cent of all amphibian species — and by definition can be as happy in water as on land. They can absorb oxygen and water through their skin and need to be kept moist, all the time.

Their major USP is that they are top class and highly sensitive indicators of the health of the environment around them and of the general well-being of their ecosystems. And of course, they inform us that global warming is happening. They certainly don't like pesticides and fertilizers mucking up their ponds and water bodies, or excessive UV radiation. More than one third of all frog species are considered threatened and as many as 120 species have gone extinct since the 1980s. Other unpleasant reminders of how badly we're treating our planet is the emergence of frightening mutations and genetic defects among them: some may have an extra leg, others may have a leg missing. Even so, new species are consistently being discovered in places like the Western Ghats and Himalayas. Our appetite for frogs' legs has led to a dangerous decline in frog populations around the world, though now that we've depleted wild stocks, frog farming for this purpose has taken off. The practice was and is barbaric: frogs are taken out of their ponds or lakes, their legs are hacked off and then their legless forms are tossed back in. We are such a pleasant species.

We've learned a lot from frogs: that, for example, of the link between electricity and the nervous system discovered by Luigi Galvani, who used the amphibians in his experiments. Galvani even used frogs' legs as a tool for measuring electric current. In 1852 a frog's heart was used by HF Stannius to show that the heart's upper chambers (atria) and lower chambers (ventricles) beat independently and at different rates.

The most glamorous and nefarious members of the froggy clan have got to be the deadly poison dart frogs of the rainforests of South and Central America. Usually tiny (less than 1.5 centimetres long) and clad in dazzling contrasting hues of scarlet, black, green, neon-blue, gold, yellow and tangerine, they are known for the toxins that ooze from their skin — making handling them (forget about eating them) very dangerous to your health. The golden poison dart frog carries enough venom to take care of between 10 and 20 men and 20,000 mice! Native Indians tipped their blow-darts with frog toxins to bring down birds and small animals. These neon-clad frogs in turn acquire their deadly defences from their diet: ants, termites, mites, centipedes, beetles — which in turn acquire the alkaloid toxins from the plants they consume. Hand-reared poison dart frogs, brought up on a non-toxic diet, become benign themselves.

We are trying use these poison dart toxins for medicinal purposes; for use in painkillers, for example. Some toxins can be 200 times as effective as morphine, but only in near-fatal doses; others are being researched for heart medication.

Frogs form an important part of the menu of several animals (including ourselves) and birds. They themselves dine on insects such as flies, grasshoppers and mosquitoes, which would otherwise run rampant. I once came across a nilgai carcass thrumming with bluebottles, busy slurping up what they could and laying their eggs. They in turn were being feasted upon by a battalion of enormous bullfrogs hopping like a lumpy moving carpet inside the opened-up ribcage of the unfortunate nilgai, feasting on meat, maggots and flies. The food chain would have been complete if the egrets and herons in attendance had had the courage to take on the frogs: but these hefty bullfrogs in their camouflage fatigues were not to be trifled with, and the birds kept their distance!

Slithery Salamanders

Salamanders can really slither around and are slippery, so difficult for predators to catch. Also, they can be poisonous, but are not venomous. This basically means if you handle one, wash your hands thoroughly because their skin secretions may be poisonous, but if they bite you, you'll be fine because they don't have venom. But they have one skillset that we can only envy and are now trying desperately to 'reverse engineer': they can regrow lost body parts, legs, tails, for example (our common house gecko also can regenerate its tail, which it sheds when it flees from enemies). We've kind of figured out that salamanders have special cells that lie just beneath the skin and which are able to develop into the type of cell required to make the replacement. Thus, those lying just beneath the skin will develop skin cells, muscle cells will develop into muscles, cartilage cells into cartilage.

If we are able to replicate this it would have awesome consequences for those unfortunates who have lost a limb or any other body part. It could also help in healing brain and spinal cord injuries. Of course, some sea creatures like sea stars, who we shall meet later, have taken this to another level — but it just shows how valuable they all are for us and the betterment of our lives. Mucking around with them and their habitats is not exactly in our best interests.

Crocs Rock!

Sadly, we really have mucked around with crocodiles, alligators and caimans: reptiles that have come down virtually unchanged since the days of the dinosaurs. Of the twenty-three species in the world three are found in our waters: the mugger or freshwater crocodile, the saltwater or estuarine crocodile and the nearly extinct gharial. With their Machiavellian grins (and that slow-motion wink) armoured hides and ferociously powerful bites, they are formidable in every way and usually the apex predators of their habitats. Apart from actively ambushing prey (anything that dares to take a drink or a swim in their waters), they scavenge on carcasses floating downstream, thus keeping the water free of dangerous bacteria. Which is more than can be said for most of us.

They may be cold-blooded, like all reptiles, but make tender mammas and some are deep-thinking too. The mugger will balance twigs on its broad forehead, knowing birds on the lookout for nesting material will pop down for a pickup and then become lunch! Just think what this involves: the croc has observed birds flying around carrying twigs. It may or may not know for what purpose. So, it makes twigs 'easily available' to them by putting them on its head! This is tool use!

We've behaved very badly with them. Until the British turned up, they were plentiful, and then till the 1970s they were hunted wholesale — for their meat and for our snazzy crocodile-leather luggage, wallets, belts and shoes. Then the Wildlife Protection Act (1972) came to their rescue — somewhat. Even until 2013 there were not more than 8,700 muggers left. Their dire numbers prompted wildlife biologist Romulus Whitaker to set up the Madras Crocodile Bank Trust near Chennai in 1975, with a view to captive-breeding and restocking water bodies where crocs had disappeared from. Captive breeding went off fine, but repatriating them back to the wild was problematic. People living near these water bodies — and using them for bathing and washing — certainly didn't want crocs in the vicinity. Everyone knew that crocs ate people, especially women and children!

Well, muggers killed eighteen people in 2018, less than what an everyday bus accident would account for, so draw your own conclusions.

The government had much the same attitude towards them: Some 300 muggers were extradited from the site where the Statue of Unity was put up, and yet another 300–500 are due to be removed from the site of the Sardar Sarovar Dam on the Narmada, where they want to set up a seaplane port. By removing apex predators from their habitat, we are unbalancing the entire ecosystem of the place and may be giving free rein to other species that may well lead to its complete ruination.

Yet, there is one village in Gujarat where people (and their children) live cheek by jowl with the crocs, bathing, washing and swimming in the same waters. In twenty-six years, there have been thirty attacks, only one fatal. Since Vedic-times crocodiles have symbolized the 'fructifying' as well as 'destructive' powers of rivers, something we will do well not to forget.

Weighing in at nearly 2 tonnes, the 23-foot-long saltwater or estuarine crocodiles ('salties') are the bad boys of the clan. They live in brackish water, some do enjoy human burgers, and they can swipe a macaque off a low overhanging branch with a swing of their mighty tails. They are not fussy eaters and can go without a meal for months, but are fiercely territorial.

In countries like Australia, 'croc wrangling' has become some kind of macho sport, all allegedly in the interests of the reptiles. First, we invade their territories, build homes and swimming pools there and then desperately shriek for help when we find a massive saltie in the pool or reclining on a poolside lounger, enjoying a pina colada, grinning at us, and saying, 'FYI, this was my place. I'm just taking it back. Thanks for the amenities, now butt out!' A gang of rednecks will turn up and the bravest will jump on the reptile's head, trying to clamp shut its fearsome jaws, followed by others who will duct tape it from snout to tail-tip — shredding it of all self-respect and dignity. Then they'll haul it off and set it 'free' in another billabong some distance away, which in a few years may also be converted into another azure swimming pool... We never learn, do we?

The crocodile which is in serious danger of extinction (status: critically endangered) is the slim, over 6 metre (nearly 20 feet) long gharial. It is armed with around 100 spiked teeth but has a bite force too weak to do any damage to us. The male sports a 'pot' or 'ghara' on its snout which serves as an echo-chamber for its love-calls, and which the ladies appear to swoon over. Around the time of independence there were thought to be 5,000 to 10,000 gharials; today the number has plunged to between 235 and 800, and these are found in just 2 per cent of the river systems they used to be.

The problem is that gharials are fussy fish-eaters and will not tolerate muck in their water. If they are present, it means the water is clean and clear. As nearly all our river systems are toxically filthy and virtually opaque, the problem becomes obvious. Also, we introduced 'tilapia' in our river systems to help the fishing industry. These bottom-feeders vacuumed up all the heavy metals and toxins in the water, and in turn were eaten by the gharial, which died in large numbers.

Captive breeding programs have been launched — for one of which apparently eggs had to be imported from Nepal at ₹ 200 a piece, and for another a gentleman gharial had to be brought over from Germany. The National Chambal Sanctuary is the reptiles' stronghold, and there is a project run by WWF India to repopulate a relatively clean section of the Beas River. Follow-up and monitoring are problematic, and often the baby gharials just get washed downstream and vanish.

The solution of course is (on paper at least) simple! Clean up the river systems and stop the muck from pouring in at the source. The gharials will tell you when the job's been done, and thank you with a toothy smile!

In Florida, golf courses have taken over the territories once held by alligators. But those gators were not going to be ousted so easily: they just remained in the water hazards of the golf courses and as long as the golfers keep a respectful distance (and don't bop them on their heads with a badly driven golf ball), coexist peacefully with them. When the gators want to waddle across the fairways and greens from one water hazard to another, the golfers just wait for them to pass. So, it just shows, with a little mutual respect and understanding, all can be well!

Turtles in the Soup

Sadly, all five of the turtle species found off our shores — the hawksbill, olive ridley, loggerhead, green and leatherback — are in trouble, taken as they are for their meat, shells (for spectacle frames!), pet trade and for totally dubious Chinese 'medicine'.

They are renowned for what's called the 'arribada' – the mass (usually) after-dark arrival of thousands of pregnant females on the very beach where they were born. Here they will now lay and bury their own eggs, before clumsily making it back to the ocean. Turtles really have the odds stacked against them: while they may live for more than 100 years, not more than one in 1,000 of their babies will make it to adulthood.

These sad-eyed, somewhat goofy looking seafarers have it tough right from birth. The tiny hatchlings must dig their way out of their nests, scamper hell-for-leather over the sand towards the ocean, instinctively guided towards it by the faint moonlight or starlight being reflected off the water and running the gauntlet of dogs, jackals, crows and humans waiting to pick them off. Even in the water, predators gather, awaiting the bonanza. What's become a major issue is that now we're confusing them with our lights – streetlights, neon-lit shops, shacks and houses near the beach – so that they often turn away from the water and head towards the land, which now has the brighter horizon and which often proves fatal for them. There is such a simple and humane solution to this problem: just switch off or dim the lights near their beaches on those few nights every year.

But once in the ocean, turtles know exactly where they are and in what direction to swim. Their tiny brains tune in to the Earth's magnetic field, assessing its angle of inclination and strength. The Earth can be likened to a massive bar magnet, with magnetic lines streaming out of the South Pole and re-entering at the North Pole. The angle of inclination will be the angle at which these lines intersect the surface of the Earth at any place, and will vary with the latitude. At the poles, the angle of inclination will be 90 degrees, at the equator, zero. Similarly, the magnetic force will be maximum at the poles and minimum at the equator.

These two readings give the turtle a sense of its bearings, and any changes in the magnetic field in the ocean will be used as navigational markers. The baby turtle will roam the ocean for decades, and if female and pregnant, will now use these markers to head back towards the very same beach she was hatched on. As she gets closer, she will 'taste' the water and follow this like a scent trail to, or near, the beach where she herself was born.

Again, we need to pause and think about this. For our GPS systems we need satellites in space, cables under the sea, huge dishes pointed skywards – an enormous amount of very expensive electronic infrastructure. The baby turtles only have their baby turtle brains. Baby turtles 1; Humans 0!

Another 'believe-it-or-not' quality turtles have: they can drink salt water (and extrude the salt through their tears), and some of their vital organs (lungs, kidneys and liver) of some species do not age. If we could get to the bottom of this…

Watching an 'arribada' should be on every nature-lover's must-do list. Happily, turtles do have friends around the world, as well as institutions such as the International Sea Turtle Society. Nature lovers and environmentalists now patrol and guard the beaches on which big mama turtles waddle up to lay their eggs and later escort the hatchlings safely to the ocean.

Snakes in the Grass

Snakes too have gotten a bad rap from us, since Biblical times. Stories abound of giant anacondas wrapping themselves around the boats of jungle explorers and swallowing them whole. And then there was Kaa in Rudyard Kipling's *Jungle Book*. Kill a naag (cobra), we say, and its wife (naagin) will have her revenge!

Many snakes are of course extremely venomous, and it is prudent to avoid them the best we can. We fear them for this but in reality, snakes are more afraid of us than we are of them. They are deaf, but highly sensitive to vibrations — of our footfalls, for instance. With us, the trouble arises when we surprise them, provoking them to attack in self-defence. In India, snakes kill around 58,000 people every year, which is a whopping toll. Many snakebite cases happen because we do not take precautions when we are in their habitats: farmers and labourers in paddy fields (a favourite haunt of cobras) wade in barefoot and can virtually step on them before

realizing
it. Where
there are rats (who love
fields and grain warehouses), there will be snakes — for
they are superlative rodent hunters. Rats account for as
much as 20 per cent of our grain stock (and in the middle
ages were responsible for spreading the Bubonic plague via
their fleas), so the contribution of snakes in controlling their
population and keeping disease at bay cannot be underestimated.
When their holes flood, snakes seek drier ground, often in the
huts of villagers, where accidents easily happen. They've come
into our cities as well, and these
days, glamorous
snake-catching
couples
in some
cities have
become
media stars
as they
rush around
pulling cobras and mambas out of
houses and schoolrooms as well as
educating locals about them. But the
best snake-catchers in the business
are the Irula tribe of Tamil Nadu, who
made a living out of snake-catching with maximum
efficiency and minimum fuss.

For long, India was known as the land of 'snake charmers', who held crowds spellbound as they made fearsome cobras sway to the music of their 'beens' or had them tangle with mongooses. Well, as just mentioned, cobras (and all snakes) are deaf; they have no outer ears, and what they were sway to is the movement of the instrument, keeping track of it in case of an attack! Most of these unfortunate cobras were defanged so even if they did strike home, they could do no harm. And we've all seen the staged (now illegal) famous 'fights' between cobra and mongoose — the only saving grace to this spectacle being that the mongoose was usually pulled away before it could deliver the killing bite, because a dead cobra would be of no use to its owner.

Many of us think of snakes as being slimy and slithery. Well, is that natty snakeskin handbag or belt of yours slimy? For eons we have hunted snakes for their lovely burnished skins — until in India the hunting of snakes was banned by the Wildlife Protection Act of 1972. This actually robbed the Irula people of their way of life until they formed the Snake Catchers' Co-operative and were recruited to catch snakes which could be milked for their venom and then released back in the wild. Venom is used to make anti-venom serum — the only way you can be saved if you are bitten by a venomous snake — a cobra, Russel's viper, saw-scaled viper or common krait (the 'big four' of India). Snake venom can paralyze us, coagulate our blood and destroy tissue in quick time, or even do a combination of these things. However, the proteins and enzymes in snake venom are being used to treat heart and renal conditions, cancer, hypertension as well as Alzheimer's and Parkinson's disease.

With their flickering forked tongues, the infra-red-heat-seeking pits near their mouths — with which they catch the scent or form a thermal image of their victims — their beady, unblinking eyes and slithery locomotion, snakes do not enamour most of us. Thankfully they have their admirers; in India people like Romulus Whitaker have done sterling work in popularizing snakes and educating the aam janta about them. In many countries, snakes — such as pythons — are captive-bred for the pet trade, sometimes to unfortunate extents; in the United States, you can keep a giant Burmese python at home and only realize you may have a problem when Junior doesn't turn up at the breakfast table in the morning! 'Pet' Burmese pythons have often been released, by people who cannot manage them anymore, in the swamps of the Florida Everglades, where they are wreaking havoc with the ecosystem — yet another instance of the smartest species on the planet behaving in the dumbest manner possible! In India, snakes are worshipped, especially during Naag Panchami, and women offer cobras milk — even if the snakes don't drink milk.

These sleek, handsome reptiles are a vital cog in the food chain. Without them, at least in India, we are likely to be overrun by rats!

CHAPTER 5:
MAGIC MUSHROOMS ET AL

W e usually only notice fungi, mushrooms and toadstools when they suddenly appear either on bread that has been left to itself for too long or after spells of rain during the monsoon, when they appear as if by magic overnight, ringing the base of a tree, or in huddled clusters in the grass or like wooden shelves on the trunks and boughs of trees.

Actually, fungi are found everywhere and their main rivals are bacteria. What we see are only the sexy parts of the organism. Most of it, called the mycelium, lies buried in the good earth – or whatever medium they are growing in. The mycelium spreads out into a mesh of narrow tubular filaments called hyphae, which expand every which way and which use enzymes to digest organic material. These hyphae extend beyond the roots of plants, reaching out from one tree to another, often exchanging minerals and information – sending this back to the trees and charging a hefty 30 per cent as fees in the form of carbon-containing materials. They go deeper into the soil than the roots and so can extract water from these depths for the trees as well.

Fungi can be invaluable to the health of a forest ecosystem, especially in this time of climate change. Mycorrhizal fungi help trees exchange carbon: trees that have a lot of carbon in their roots may via these fungi transfer this carbon to trees that have less. Thanks to the effects of climate change — wildfires, floods, heatwaves and drought — many trees are put under huge stresses. It's being suspected now (and experiments are being carried out to confirm if this is indeed so) that trees which are 'stronger' (i.e., richer in carbon) may help 'weaker' trees (i.e., poorer in carbon) by donating carbon to them during these hard times, and thus help them survive. (Like you would do if you donated blood to someone who was highly anaemic or had just lost a lot of blood.) Overall, this would help in fostering a healthy forest ecosystem, which in turn would purify water, emit more oxygen

and help regulate and cool the climate, thus slowing down the rate of climate change.

But for me, the biggest takeaway is this: if (strong) trees can help (weak) trees in keeping climate change in check by giving them carbon, why the heck can't we help each other? Why can't developed countries give enough help to developing countries (which they have royally ripped off anyway) to reduce emissions and improve technology so that we can all live in a more equitable environment? Why can't our 'carbon markets' behave more in this manner? When will we ever learn?

We all also know of at least one invaluable fungus: that belonging to the genus Penicillium. It has been used in the manufacture of Penicillin, the ubiquitous antibiotic that has saved millions of lives the world over. So we can never underestimate the value of fungi. Another very useful duty performed is that like bacteria, fungi break down dead organic material, recycling them back into the ecosystem. Nature does not believe in a throwaway society. Yeast is yet another invaluable member of this group. We would not have fragrant loaves of bread or croissants, or beer for that matter, without it, and life really wouldn't be worth living then! Yeast breaks down sugar into carbon dioxide and alcohol, and it is this gas that makes a loaf rise in the oven.

Truffles (formal name Tuber melanosporum), found in France, make foodies swoon — and are sniffed out from their underground lairs beneath oak trees by specially bred truffle-hounds or pigs. Like caviar they are considered the Rolls-Royces of their family.

And then of course, there are the bewildering and colourful variety of mushrooms and toadstools, many of which are so tempting to pluck from a hillside forest and stir-fry in a little butter... But you really have to know your mushrooms because many are cruelly toxic. Though antidotes are available, by the time you realize you've been poisoned it's too late. They can cause coma, paralysis and death — they destroy your vital organs like the liver and kidneys. Fortunately, mushrooms are grown commercially and these are of course completely safe and very nourishing and delicious! It is well known that some mushrooms, like those of the fly agaric can send you on psychedelic hallucinogenic trips, which several rockstars have been known to indulge in to give their fans something really to rock to during their concerts!

There's yet another species of fungi which has another 'magic trick' up its sleeve. Trichoderma viridae, better known as green mold, is a garden biofungicide used to fight harmful fungi in soil. This one has an enzyme that can also break down normally indigestible cellulose (found in wood) into its constituent glucose molecules. And it can do this even with old newspapers (paper comes from wood, wood comes from trees...), producing high yields of sugar. The printing ink on the newspaper and other stuff used to make the paper are turned into a black sludge that settles morosely at the bottom of the container, while the top is filled with sweet syrup!

Truly diabolical, however, is the popularly called 'zombie-ant fungus', (Ophicordyceps unilateralis) found in tropical and semi-tropical rainforests and first discovered by Darwin's contemporary, Alfred Russell Wallace, back in 1859. These like the temperature to be between 20 and 30 degrees Celsius, with 94 to 95 per cent humidity, so global warming is something they might just look forward to! If you were a carpenter ant with the family name Camponotini, you'd do well to keep away from the spores of this one by staying up in your nests in the tree canopy. Because if one of the spores of this fungus adheres to you (and they are sticky, to be found on the forest floor, where you may happen to be trundling along, perhaps to climb up another tree) you're well and truly a 'dead ant walking'.

The filaments (hyphae) of the spores will secrete enzymes and, using sheer mechanical force, drill through your exoskeleton to enter your body. Now the spores will head for your nervous and circulatory systems, playing havoc with your genes, your muscles and your mind. They'll suppress your immune system, make you wander around aimlessly, ignore your colleagues in the colony and eventually cause convulsions that make you fall out of your treetop nest to the ground. Bemused, bewitched and bewildered, you'll head for the nearest small plant and climb up to a stem or leaf about 25 inches off the ground and face north. And now, the zombie fungus will make you bite into the leaf or stem like you've never bitten before, so hard that once your mandibles clamp down, they'll be locked tight forever and ever. You'll be hanging by them from the leaf, or stem, but mercifully will die very soon after you take this fatal bite. The fungi will now feed on you from the inside, and then the final humiliation – send fruiting bodies right through your head into the open air like a victory salutation. These will rupture and send yet more spores into the big, beautiful world, to continue their good work with more of your brethren!

A video game series called *The Last of Us* was based on this macabre theme. But take heart: so far at least, the fungus does not infect humans, but then who knows what the future (and fungus) and global warming holds! They are weird and wonderful and may hold secret powers, and they need to be handled with a healthy amount of caution and respect.

CHAPTER 6: YOU MUST GO DOWN TO THE SEAS

Our oceans and seas remain the most unexplored (and major) portion of our potpourri planet, and with the oceans gradually heating up, the myriad life forms that have made the oceans their homes face an uncertain future. Cold waters hold more nutrients, on which a host of creatures depend, and with the water temperatures rising, these have to go further north to find enough to eat. Ocean currents too are affected by warming waters, and the melting of sea ice at the poles will eventually mean that coastal cities (no matter how much they bulwark their shores) will eventually, if gradually, drown. Several pancake-flat low-lying islands — like the Maldives in the Indian Ocean and others in the Pacific Ocean — are most at risk, as are larger countries such as Bangladesh.

Pollution is another weapon of mass destruction that we have let loose on the oceans. Tankers spill vast quantities of oil when they hit rocks or capsize, or simply when they illegally flush their tanks in the water, leaving huge shoals of dead fish, whales, dolphins and seabirds miserably glinting with oil, unable to fly or eat, in their toxic wake. Oil slicks spread like stains of evil over vast areas of aquamarine sea. Expensive clean-up operations have to be launched as the tides purge balls of oil and tar on pristine beaches. The Great Pacific Garbage Patch, which is as large as Alaska, floats between Hawaii and the Californian coast, a disgusting mess of plastic jetsam and flotsam: empty shampoo bottles, jerry cans, packaging material and nylon fishing nets, between 45,000 and 129,000 tonnes of it. We dump some 8 million tonnes of garbage into the oceans every year. Discarded or abandoned fishing nets strangle sharks and sea turtles.

Way back in 2011, an eighteen-year-old Dutch student by the name of Boyan Slat was appalled by the amount of plastic waste he encountered when he went diving off the coast of Greece. There was more plastic than fish, he claimed. From aerospace engineering he turned his attention to cleaning up the filthy seas. In 2013, he formed the non-profit organization 'The Ocean Clean Up' and devised basically what was a huge floating semi-circular net-like device, which would scoop up the floating plastic trash and take it to the shore, where it could be dealt with, or segregate and process it in situ. There were several technical hiccups that had to be overcome, and as of 2022 a new contraption called 'The Interceptor' has been deployed in Indonesia, Malaysia and the Dominican Republic (with other countries on the waitlist). This barge-like system is solar-powered and can be resized according to need. The idea is to have the Interceptors placed not only in the ocean, but at the mouths of the major-polluting rivers. A thousand of the major river systems in the world (including the Ganges) are apparently responsible for 80 per cent of the world's plastic pollution, so it's clear how useful this device would be in 'shutting off the taps' as it were.

Microplastics are everywhere — including in the digestive tracts of most aquatic creatures. For centuries, we've used the oceans as a vast dumping ground for sewage and industrial waste. The missiles being tested by most nations eventually all fall into the seas, and I wonder about the effect they must have in the splashdown zone. You wouldn't like this to happen in your neck of the woods (or in your swimming pool!), certainly. Walk on nearly any beach in India and you will be disgusted by the vast number of plastic bottles, bags, jerry cans, broken bottles, torn nylon netting and even diapers, not to mention early-morning offerings of the local populace, that float in with the waves or stud the sandy shores.

Most of us, alas, are unable to dive down deep into the ocean to have a look at the strange, magical and truly wondrous creatures that dwell there — but there are enough shallow-water dwellers to keep us spellbound for a lifetime, when we beachcomb. But tread carefully, for several of these dwellers are viciously venomous. Others have magical qualities.

Superstars All

Take starfish, for example. You can sometimes find these washed up on the beach near the low-tide mark. There are around 1,600 species of starfish in the world; they sport between five and fifty arms, which radiate out of a central hub. Now, the starfish seems to be a great believer in free thinking, because each of its arms is more or less an independent entity. Thus, if one arm wishes to travel in one direction (it is equipped by suction-causing tubular feet, which work hydraulically) and a second in another, it takes a while before the central hub (like the government at the centre) can decide in which direction the starfish must move, because there is no central nervous system.

Cut off, or bite off, an arm of a starfish and it will merely shrug and in a short while grow another. If you spit out the arm you bit off, it may even grow into a brand-new starfish altogether. One species, (Californian, needless to say!) even reproduces this way (asexually), by simply splitting itself in to two. But when starfish make out, the lady can produce up to 2.5 million eggs, though few survive. Even so, the crown-of-thorns starfish (one of the largest) has gained notoriety for decimating coral reefs like the Great Barrier Reef off Australia, because of population explosions. One reason cited is that we have considerably reduced the numbers of their predators – like tritons (a beautiful sea snail), which have been taken by collectors. Other reasons include the habitat destruction of their other predators, the warming of the oceans, which assist larval growth, and even the fact that taking a bite out of a starfish may not be enough to kill it as it just regrows the chewed-off part! Fishermen who feared for the security of their oyster beds (on which starfish preyed) plucked them out, cut them up and threw them back in the water – only to increase their population even more as the broken bits just regrew into new starfish!

Their cousins, the brittle stars that live on the ocean beds, work like a scavenging service, ridding the water of organic waste, and glory be they love polluted water!

Cleansing Cucumbers

Another astonishing deep-sea living 'regenerator' is the sea cucumber. It too plays an important role in recycling nutrients and breaking down organic waste, which is then further decomposed by bacteria. One specimen can ingest as much as 45 kilograms of sediment a year and eject it in a finer, purer form. When threatened they turn inside-out via their anus, some smothering their predators with a toxic substance, which would be like being crapped upon with some kind of poisonous shit! For the sea cucumber however, it's a wonderful way of saying, 'You disgust me!', or rejecting an indecent proposal!

Reefwreck!

Coral reefs have been at the centre of attention of scuba divers and snorkelers for ages, for their shimmering beauty and the kaleidoscopic life forms they support in shallow tropical seas. They take care of a quarter of all marine life forms, including sponges, clams, oysters, crabs, sea urchins and sea stars, as well 4,000 species of fish, which are dependent on them in one way or another. The Taj Mahal of coral reefs is of course the Great Barrier Reef off the north-eastern coast of Australia, which stretches for over 2,000 kilometres into the Pacific Ocean. This magnificent underwater mountain range has 'peaks' that peep out of the ocean in the form of coral islands and reefs (which can be dangerous to ships). A coral reef may be over 450 metres thick in places and yet is as fragile as a disgruntled teenager in the early morning.

Astonishingly, this massive structure has been designed and built by tiny animals, each no larger than a match-head: the coral polyps. Each coral polyp is somewhat like an anemone, except that it builds a strong chalky skeleton over its body, into which it can retract when danger threatens. Reef corals are nocturnal diners; during the day they retire inside their skeletons, looking boring. But it's at night that they come out (and dress up) to dine: stretching out vivid poison-barbed tentacles and looking like swaying beds of chrysanthemums. Sunlight and clear water are essential to the growth of corals, because there is a vital association between the coral and minute algae: zooxanthellae, which live in the cells of the coral tissue. The algae, capable of photosynthesis, provide food (organic carbon products) for the coral — meeting as much as 90 per cent of the coral's energy needs via photosynthesis — and help it to extract calcium from the water for its skeleton. In return the coral provides nutrients, carbon dioxide and a place near the sunlight to enable photosynthesis to take place! Murky, sediment-clouded water would choke the tiny polyps, rendering them incapable of feeding, and prevent enough sunlight from permeating through for photosynthesis to take place effectively.

Coral reefs are very fussy entities: they don't like the water either too hot or too cold. If the sea gets too warm, even by just 1 degree Celsius, the zooxanthellae produce reactive oxygen types, like peroxides, which are toxic for the coral. So, it expels the zooxanthellae. The coral polyps begin to bleach, or go white, because it is the algae that give the corals their colour. The coral polyp itself turns transparent, leaving its chalky white calcium carbonate skeleton behind. Also, it begins to slowly starve, because it is not very good at gathering food for itself and, as mentioned, depends on the algae for 90 per cent of its energy requirements and nourishment. If the water

begins to cool down again, the zooxanthellae may be readmitted by the coral polyps and regular service, and food supplies, may resume. If not, the coral dies; its skeleton is engulfed by bacteria, effectively blocking any chances of recovery. And when the corals die, the ecosystems dependent on them begin to decline and eventually die out too. There is a loss of diversity in the species of fish, especially niche species, which in turn affects coral health and well-being, as also depriving fishers of a living: it is estimated that there has been a 44 per cent decline in fish populations in the Florida Keys and as much as an 80 per cent decline in the Caribbean because of this. Many commercial fish species spawn in and around coral reefs, and their young grow up here, thanks to the protection coral reefs offer. One study has estimated that the losses incurred due to coral bleaching could be anywhere between $49 and $69 billion if we do not reduce our greenhouse gas emissions! And worse, the countries that will be hit hardest are the developing countries where the reefs are located: in Southeast Asia and the Indian Ocean.

Like mangroves and swaying beds of seagrass, and kelp, coral reefs also provide protection to coasts from the rampages of an angry ocean, preventing and reducing the erosion of the shores and flooding.

Global warming due to ever increasing carbon dioxide emissions is of course one of the major factors leading to higher sea temperatures and coral bleaching. Other factors include increasing sedimentation, too much ultraviolet radiation, the presence of non-biodegradable chemicals used in sunscreen washing off the bodies of swimmers and surfers, an increase in ocean acidification due to higher carbon dioxide levels resulting from air pollution, pollutants in the water and changes in water chemistry. Cyanide fishing, herbicides and dust blown over due to drought on continents like Africa also add to the reef's trauma. Dredging and blasting and drilling for sandstone, minerals and water near reefs are, needless to say, devastating for the reefs, as is crude oil spillage from tankers. Tourists with their speedboats also damage these fragile reefs.

Mass bleaching events have risen sharply since the early 1980s, worldwide: in 2016 bleaching in the Great Barrier Reef killed between 29 and 50 per cent of the reef's coral and according to a National Geographic report, between 2013 and 2016, three quarters of the world's reef systems suffered from severe bleaching. Once a reef dies, it is next to impossible to regenerate it, though we have come up with some ingenious solutions to 'grow' new reefs: cement, steel and limestone have been used, as have old tyres and cinder blocks. An old ship has even been sunk to form an artificial reef (shipwrecks make very good artificial reefs), as have (ironically) oil-drilling platforms and lighthouses.

Not all corals live in warm, shallow waters. There are about as many species of shallow-water corals as there are of deep-sea corals, which can be found as deep as 6,000 metres under the sea. So far, some 3,300 species have been discovered and the count is rising! They too can live singly (as polyps), or in colonies, in a bewildering variety of shapes, sizes and colours. Unlike their shallow-dwelling cousins, they are not dependent on zooxanthellae for their sustenance, but obtain it from trapping tiny organisms from the passing currents. They are found in all of the earth's oceans and can live in waters as cold as −1 degree Celsius. They too provide homes, hunting grounds and nurseries to a vast variety of marine life, from worms, starfish, to deep sea fish. And they have long lives: one black coral has been estimated to be 4,265 years old and as coral polyps regenerate continuously, some reefs have been alive for 40,000 years.

A coral reef and our beaches at low tide, be they rocky or sandy, or in the icy depths, are wondrous ecosystems and are inhabited by some truly dazzling creatures, from tiny to gargantuan. Many of them have a unique USP, which makes them extra-special. So let me introduce you to a few of these creatures here. Some, like jellyfish and sea anemones, are deemed 'soft' corals. (These are usually less sensitive about the temperature of the water.)

Of Pain and Poison

One of the most common creatures usually encountered on our beaches during the monsoons is the shimmering purple and green Portuguese man o' war. It looks something like a small flaccid plastic balloon, tinted an inky purple-blue. Beware! It is well-armed with numerous venomous explosive stinging tentacles and even while looking (and being) dormant and dead on the sand is dangerous. Its venom is powerful enough to inflict a great deal of pain and even kill a human. Not a jellyfish but like one, it comprises an entire community of organisms made up of individual units called zooids. Each zooid (genetically identical to every other one) is a specialist – while one might be responsible for feeding, another may be in charge of reproduction, all of them together operating cooperatively and functioning as a single entity (unlike political parties).

The Portuguese man o' war have no independent means of locomotion but depend on the wind and tides to take them where they will. Their inflated 'plastic bags', which are filled with carbon monoxide and air, serve as sails, making them look like the sailing warships of yore, thus giving them their moniker. Not much is known about these deadly floaters as they bob across the oceans, trailing their venom-barbed tentacles behind to snare, paralyze and reel in small fish, fish fry and plankton. They are subject to severe ultraviolet radiation, desiccation and the violent rock-and-roll of the waves and have devised one truly ingenious survival tactic. Their floats are either oriented to the right or to the left, usually in a 50:50 ratio. Those with a right-side orientation will float towards the left, and the 'lefties' will float to the right. Thus, when being buffeted towards a beach, half of them may be stranded on the sand, while the other half may be pushed in the opposite direction, ensuring the survival of at least half the population. These dangerous entities are predated upon by loggerhead turtles (who are too thick-skinned for the tentacles to penetrate), as well as violet snails and the blanket octopus, whose young actually carry around snapped off tentacles and use them for their own offensive attacks, or in defence!

One of the deadliest of all sea creatures is the notorious box jellyfish, especially at home in the waters off the coast of northern Australia. Bluish as a gas flame, and semi-transparent, these cuboid shaped bag-like entities may be 25 centimetres across and trail fifteen poison-tipped tentacles, each one metre long, from each of their four 'corners'. Each tentacle is armed with up to 5,000 stinging hook-barbed capsules that can kill you in minutes through sheer pain and shock — causing you to drown — apart from causing heart failure and attacking your nervous system and skin cells. Unlike the Portuguese man o' war, box jellyfish can propel themselves at up to 4 knots, and have twenty-four eyes arranged in clusters around the bell. Some can only distinguish light and shade, others have sight similar to that in higher animals. But scientists still don't know exactly how they process vision as the jellyfish lack a central nervous system!

Sea Shells on the Seashore

We've all at some time collected shells on the beach, or bought them in the market — a practice that is now discouraged or has been made illegal. Usually, the original owner and builder (a sea snail) has either vacated, been eaten or died. But some of these erstwhile owners, like those of the textile cone shells, are not to be trifled with: they prowl around at the bottom of the reef, and are armed with a venomous, backward toothed harpoon, which they shoot out at prey — small fish — and reel them in. The venom, apart from causing excruciating pain, can also kill us.

In the past, cowries were used as currency and even now, we use the conch 'shankh' for religious rituals. I have myself a small collection of shells gathered from beaches in Madras and Bombay decades ago and even now marvel at the patterns, colours, diversity and sheer architecture of some of them: some resemble spires and cathedral domes, and even ice cream cones! While the outer part of a shell is made of calcium carbonate, the inner lining is made of a substance called nacre, or mother of pearl, which we use for jewellery making. Acidification of the oceans eats into the shells, killing their owners. Sea snails, oysters (with the lure of a pearl), mussels and scallops have been eaten by us for eons: Roman soldiers on the march kept sea snails in their tunic pockets as an on-the-go energy provider, rather like an energy bar! Escargots (a fancy name for snails) and oysters are served at fancy restaurants all over the world, and oyster 'farming' is big business.

Skedaddlers on the Sand

The other common occupants of any beach are crabs. Ghost and soldier crabs shimmy disdainfully into the sand as you approach, vanishing in a trice (and considerably puzzling nosey parker dogs). They feed by filtering minute life forms and nutrients out of the sand, leaving attractive little blobs of sand arranged in rangoli-like patterns on the beach. My favourite is the hermit crab which, strictly speaking, is not really a crab, being more closely related to lobsters. There are some 500 species, many of which (including the massive, powerful coconut or robber crab) are terrestrial — though they all have to come down to the sea to spawn. Normally crabs, and other 'crustaceans', as this clan is known, have a hard exoskeleton or carapace (shell) covering their entire bodies. The carapace of the hermit crabs is somewhat incomplete, leaving it with a soft, exposed bottom, and an invitation for predators to take a bite. To protect its vulnerable rear-end, the hermit crab finds and carefully backs into the discarded shell of a snail or periwinkle. It must fit just right. Too small and it obviously won't be able to squeeze into it and too large means it will be rattling around in a mansion so large that it becomes easy for a predator to insert a tentacle into it and drag the poor occupant out. Something in this for us to think about: do we really need twenty-seven-storey buildings for a family of six, or 200-bedroom palaces for just two people?

But what's really astonishing is the way hermit crabs find the right accommodation. Say we have a crab that has outgrown its present accommodation and needs to upsize. It crawls out (and is now naked and afraid) and finds a discarded shell. But this one is far too large for it. So it goes back home and simply hangs around outside the discarded mansion. Soon enough another hermit looking for property (hermit crabs are always on the lookout for property) trundles up – it is a little larger than the first one, but still too small for the palatial mansion. So, it too waits. More property seekers turn up and like Brits at a bus stop neatly queue up, the largest at the top of the line and smallest at the end, in front of the mansion. At last, a big fellow turns up, for whom the mansion is a perfect fit. It crawls out of its shell and settles into it. Now its shell (smaller than the mansion) is vacant and the waiting crabs now kind of break up their queue trying to figure out who will fit nicely into this newly vacated home. But eventually they sort things out and one by one, as homes are vacated and filled according to size, each one gets a shell that fits it right.

I met my first hermit crab on Morjim beach in Goa. It had rented a long spiral-shaped shell and when I picked it up, peeked at me out of huge, expressive eyes. Obviously horrified at who was at its door (a Dilliwalla, no less) it ducked back in promptly, shutting the door in my face as if I were a shoe salesman or realtor. I put it back on the beach. If you must collect shells on the beach – it would be better if you didn't, because there's a shortage of housing in hermit-crab society – it would be courteous to first check if the shell is occupied.

The housing shortage in hermit-crab society is really quite serious, and plastic pollution is playing havoc with innocent hermit-crab property seekers. Sometimes hermit crabs mistake plastic bottle caps or containers for a possible home. One study found that as many as 570,000 hermit crabs die annually by getting trapped in plastic debris, in just two South Pacific islands. When they die, selflessly they release a pheromone advertising that a home may be available, unwittingly inviting more hermits into what is ultimately a death trap.

The decorator crab does something a little different. It uses what it can find in its immediate surroundings to camouflage itself. It might use shells, plants, pebbles, grains of sand and other debris from its environment, in order to meld into the background as it were. If you were to put one in an aquarium with a handful of multi-coloured beads, they would stick these on to their shells and trundle about happily! Sometimes they use toxic creatures, like anemones, which give them protection. In return, the anemone gets the bits of food that break off or are discarded by the crab.

More Precious than Pearls

One's first reaction to the word 'oysters' is of course pearls. They're also a delicacy in many parts of the world, eaten raw or cooked. Oysters do create pearls and have superpower elements like zinc and selenium and amino acids that bump up testosterone levels in gentlemen: they are aphrodisiac! As for pearls, well they're nothing by layers of nacre (literally, mother of pearl) which have been wrapped around a particle that somehow has got into the oyster and irritated the heck out of it. Nacre is really nothing more than a bio-mineral form of calcium carbonate called aragonite. As most of us love shiny things, we deliberately insert the irritants into oysters and later 'harvest' the shells. This is a huge business, never mind the discomfort caused to the oysters.

But all this really pales into insignificance in relation to what oysters do in their underwater environment. They are VIP entities, what we call a 'keystone' species on which the health and well-being of entire undersea ecosystems depends. They are water purification units par excellence. With the help of fine hair like structures called cilia, they take in turgid sea water and filter out plankton and dissolved organic particles, and consume nitrogen-containing compounds (nitrates and ammonia) as well as phosphates and bacteria from the water, leaving it clear and clean. What they don't use as food they expel as pellets — these eventually biodegrade into nitrogen, which enters the atmosphere. A single oyster is capable of filtering up to 190 litres of water per day, so you can see how effective an entire oyster bed or reef would be as a giant filtration system. We have recognized this immense 'green service' and are (and certainly ought to be) restoring oyster reefs all around the world.

The upper 'shell' of the oyster — which is a bivalve — is rough, and provides nooks and crannies for many tiny sea creatures, such as sea anemones, mussels and barnacles, to take sanctuary in. Some oysters can be as large as a dinner plate, so there is plenty of space for any asylum seekers.

Sadly, like nearly every living creature on this potpourri planet, oysters have issues with us. Overfishing in some parts of the world is one, another is the undersea low-frequency sounds, caused by the propellers of giant ships, or pile drivers and the explosions caused by oil (and other) exploration on the ocean beds. These disturb them considerably and may cause behavioural changes in them.

Scattered on the rocks on a beach in Goa I came across what I first took to be the white droppings of some large seabird. It turned out that they were possibly oyster shells. There was of course no sign of the oysters themselves, let alone any pearls! I have never eaten oysters so cannot tell you what they taste like, or what, if any, effect they have, but they're known to be low in calories and high on proteins. Aficionados roll up their eyes in bliss as they 'shuck' oysters and pop them into their mouths, others claim that it's like eating snot! Which, really, is not a nice thing to say about an animal that spends its life cleaning up the mucky seabed and keeping its environment healthy and its denizens happy. That is so much more than what most of us are doing!

Undersea Einsteins: Octopuses

Octopuses, which can be found both in the shallows (even in the intertidal zone of the polluted Juhu beach in Mumbai) or in the mysterious deeps, are regarded as the Einsteins of the oceans. They inhabit coral reefs, intertidal zones, pelagic waters and the seabed. With their large domed heads, two forward-facing eyes and powerful sucker-tipped tentacles, they have been regarded by some as alien creatures. Ever since Jules Verne wrote *Twenty Thousand Leagues Under the Sea* they've also been deemed to be sea monsters with a reputation of engulfing entire ships in their tentacles and taking them down. Thankfully,

their reputation was restored by Craig Foster in his remarkable 2020 documentary *My Octopus Teacher*, which shone a very different light on these astonishing animals. It's most likely that octopuses are sentient.

All octopuses are venomous, the blue-ringed octopus especially so – its venom can kill human beings. But octopuses use their venom to subdue their prey – fish, crustaceans, sting rays and the like. After engulfing their victim they draw it to them and, with their sharp beak, just beneath that domed forehead, dispatch it. They are solitary animals, only getting together to make out – after which, the male dies and the female lays her eggs in a concealed crevice, guards them zealously till they hatch and then fades away herself. They may themselves be preyed upon by sharks and large fish, and use their siphons to jet away from them, releasing a cloud of ink in their wake to blind them.

These very intelligent animals have extremely complex nervous systems with 168 types of protocadherins (proteins which enable neurons to make connections with each other) as against our own fifty-eight, so they're really wired up. In addition, they can also regenerate lost arms, and change their colour in seconds so that they merge with their surroundings. Each of their eight arms has a brain of its own, independent of the brain in that big domed head. In some countries scientists experimenting on them are not allowed to do so unless the animals are anaesthetized; this is because they are hyperaware of the resulting pain.

And they have given scientists the world over a run for their money. They are escape-artistes par excellence, slithering out of their tanks and vanishing down drains magically, and are able to work out problems in order to get what they want. Their soft boneless bodies enable them to squeeze through the narrowest of gaps and literally ooze their way out. We certainly still have a lot to learn from them and, as Craig Foster so movingly showed, can make friends with them too. That could indeed change our lives in a very happy way!

While wandering around on a beach you may have come across an oval-shaped white disc, slightly convex at the centre, with a brittle, parchment-like texture, lying on the sand. It was most probably a cuttlebone, whose dead owner was a cuttlefish and a rival to the octopus in the intelligence stakes! The cuttlebone — also made of aragonite (calcium carbonate) — actually served as a floating device for the cuttlefish, adjusting the gas to liquid ratio in it through its porous surface, thus increasing or decreasing the density of the cuttlefish, depending on whether it wanted to dive down or come up in the water. Thanks to their rich calcium content cuttlebones are regularly fed to caged birds (like budgerigars), shrimp, hermit crabs, reptiles and snails. It can withstand high temperatures and is thus also used for making small metal castings for jewellery making.

Though they cannot see in colour cuttlefish have very sophisticated eyes, with W-shaped pupils, and can discern polarized light, which enhances contrast and sharpness. Cuttlefish too are past masters at swiftly changing their colour and texture depending upon the circumstances and surroundings. They hunt crustaceans, mollusks, small fish, oysters, octopus and even other cuttlefish with the help of their sucker-equipped eight arms and two tentacles. They're basically shallow water animals found in tropical and temperate seas, though they may even be met at depths of 600 metres. So far, they do not seem to be in danger (according to the IUCN Red List of Threatened Species) though with increasing carbon dioxide levels and the warming of the oceans, the future for them remains unknown.

Let the Seagrass Sing!

Swaying, wavy green beds of sea grasses actually have slender grass-like leaves and, like all plants, have roots, stems, flowers, seeds and leaves. They live in shallow brackish waters from the tropics to the Arctic Circle, sometimes in the form of lovely green meadows which support a host of sea creatures from tiny invertebrates to marine mammals and birds. There are so vital to the well-being of their environment that they've been called ecosystem engineers, because they tune their habitats to make them better not only for themselves but for other creatures that depend on them as well.

One square metre of seagrass can generate 10 litres of oxygen every day through photosynthesis (they're called the lungs of the sea), and they also help take carbon dioxide out of the atmosphere, absorbing it like terrestrial plants and storing the carbon to make their leaves and stems. It's been estimated that the world's seagrass meadows can hoard away 83 million metric tonnes of carbon every year. (Others with similar abilities include salt marshes and mangroves.) Also, much of the nutrients and fertilizers and run-off we pour into the ocean is absorbed by them, leaving the waters glassy-clear and pure. Conversely, in nutrient-poor areas, they absorb whatever little nutrients there are and release them into the water through their leaves, thus working as a nutrient pump.

And they make wonderful hosts! A single acre of seagrass can host more than 40,000 fish and 50 million small invertebrates. Many species of fish are born and raised in the safety of seagrass beds. Crabs, lobsters, mollusks, sponges, clams, sea anemones et al., all get board-and-lodging in the seagrass beds, and large mammals such as dugongs and manatees graze peacefully on the leaves. Dugongs can go through 40 kilograms of seagrass a day, and sea-turtles, 2 kilograms — both these species are endangered because of habitat destruction.

Epiphytes too grow on seagrass leaves, some of which can absorb nitrogen from the atmosphere and make it available to larger animals. Others provide food for tiny crustaceans, which help to clean the leaves and have been called 'housekeepers'. These in turn are eaten by larger crustaceans such as crabs as well as fish. Even when dead, the decomposed leaves support a host of decomposers which thrive on the dead and rotting!

Naturally we have taken advantage of seagrasses, in fact for more than 10,000 years. They've been used as fertilizers, as thatch for roofs, to make furniture and even to stuff car seats! Fishermen flock to them, knowing that the fishing will be good amidst these swaying green meadows.

But, like most other ecosystems on earth, they are under the gun. It's thought that we're losing 5 per cent of seagrass coverage worldwide every year — that's around two football fields every hour. There is direct damage from powerful waves and storms (which are increasing in ferocity due to global warming), and dredging. Excess run-off of pollutants and nutrients from our activities cause algal bloom, which blocks the sunlight and prevents photosynthesis, thus killing off the plants. As the seas warm, the seagrass become stressed, breathing out more carbon dioxide than the oxygen they produce through photosynthesis. Warmer waters mean that the seagrasses need even more sunlight and affect how quickly they can absorb nutrients, which in turn makes them prone to disease. In the last hundred years, we've lost nearly a third of the planet's seagrass meadows. We can ill-afford to lose more.

Seaweeds aka macroalgae were among the earliest forms of life and responsible for the evolution of all green plants on earth — so we owe them big time. Apart from being very good for your health (for the Japanese they are what bread is to the French!) they can actually cool the oceans and mitigate climate change. Some fifty million years ago (in the Eocene age), a seaweed-like fern called Azolla absorbed such significant amounts of carbon dioxide (and emitted oxygen) that it actually cooled the earth to the extent of triggering off an Ice Age, wherein the annual mean temperature plummeted from 9 degrees Celsius to −9 degrees! According to scientists if just 9 per cent of the oceans were covered with seaweed, they would absorb more greenhouse gases that we currently emit.

The Sea Is Not Soup!

Warming oceans are also posing a threat to the famous 'sardine runs' which occur mainly up the south-east coast of Africa. Every winter vast shoals of sardines, maybe 10 million strong, migrate up the east-coast of Africa from South Africa, right up to the port city of Durban, a distance of some 2000 kilometres, pursued by tens of thousands of dolphins, a thousand sharks and 100,000 seabirds, not to mention fishers and tourists. The catch is that the sardines can't tolerate water temperatures above 20 degrees Celsius, and thanks to global warming, the seas have become warmer, and consequently, the sardines don't 'run', causing a devastating domino effect on the other creatures (and their young) which depended on them for sustenance. Nor does it seem that the sardines are happy with churning, turbulent, murky waters which are a result of the ever more frequent cyclones and storms that have been roiled up by global warming.

We've been steadily warming our oceans and seas ever since the Industrial Revolution, through the hugely increased use of fossil fuels and consequent emissions of carbon dioxide and methane. The ocean absorbs much of this heat as well – as much as 25 per cent of the increase in human-emitted carbon dioxide. This in turn leads to the acidification of the ocean, which affects marine life detrimentally (like crustaceans, mollusks and more importantly zooplankton, which form the base of the oceanic food chain, and whose shells get weaker). The warmer water remains near the surface, while the cold water remains deep below. Also, the reduced mixing of warm and cold water means that the water at the surface is soon unable to absorb yet more heat and this has to be accommodated by the atmosphere and the land, which in turn, now supercharged with excess energy, dispense this in the form of extreme weather events such as hurricanes, cyclones and ferocious storms. Warmer surface water also holds less nutrients, thus affecting marine life — and the quantity of fish available to us.

There are somewhere between 34,000 and 35,000 species of both marine and freshwater fish, from sardines and mackerel, to kingfish, pomfret, rays, salmon and sharks in our oceans, rivers and lakes, many of which support a gargantuan fishing industry the world over. In addition, there are sea mammals, from dolphins, porpoises and manatees to humungous whales as well as seals (of various species), and the iconic polar bear. The warming of the oceans affects and threatens their lives and their migratory travels: the melting of sea ice in the Arctic has meant that polar bears have to scrounge and scavenge for food such as seabirds and eggs from rocky shorelines and cliffs and our garbage bins and dumps, rather than hunt seals on the sea ice, which is what they were born to do. In winter when polar bears hibernate, they do so in dens under the snow, where mama bears give birth. With the snow melting earlier, the dens suffer from roof collapses, killing the cubs, or the cubs are brought out into the open by their concerned mother, much before they are ready to come out into the big bad world — and they perish.

There are thus cracks in the food chain in our oceans, which have caused changes in where the fish can be found and in what numbers, and which in turn affect our fishing industry. It causes overfishing in many areas and practices like deep-sea trawling by major fishing conglomerates, which pillage the ocean and ocean beds, often wasting huge amounts of what they call by-catch – and robbing small, traditional fishers of their livelihoods.

We've been gleaning sequestered carbon from the ocean beds in the form of crude oil and gas for decades now. Whether it is the North Sea, or our own offshore oil rigs in the Arabian Sea or Bay of Bengal, it is indeed ironic and a bit tragic that we've been taking out from the ocean something that it had sequestered safely away from us, and are then burning it up again, in our vehicles and industries, to foul up our skies and heat up our seas, in a mindless cycle of ultimate self-abuse.

Warming oceans and melting ice caps naturally mean rising sea levels, which is not good news for low-lying countries like Bangladesh, islands and coastal cities like Mumbai, Chennai, New York and London. A few islands in the Pacific have already been submerged, and have had to be evacuated. The Maldives is one such island in the Indian Ocean which appears to be next in the firing line.

The seas and oceans are a kaleidoscopic, wondrous, largely unexplored realm – the largest, most important ecosystem on our potpourri planet, from which we have a lot to glean and discover. As we've seen some of its denizens are truly remarkable, from photosynthesizing zooids to Einstein-like octopuses to astonishing and deadly box jellyfish. To destroy this and them would be to destroy ourselves, in spirit, soul and body. We need to cool down our world, and quickly. We must go down to the seas again.

CHAPTER 7: OPEN SKIES

I first got interested in birds several decades ago, when I saw a dumpy green coppersmith barbet, dressed like a clown, hiccupping away on a peepul tree in Mumbai, through a pair of brand-new 10X50 binoculars. There are around 1,200 species of birds in India (and around 10,000 worldwide) and I wondered what they looked like and what kind of shenanigans they got up to. I'm still finding out and remain both bewildered and astonished with the talents they possess and the strategies they adapt to live and fly on.

Birds have made us extremely envious: they can fly when and where they want (without recourse to passports, visas, tickets and huge, roaring, carbon-dioxide-spewing aircrafts) – and we can't. Of course, insects can fly too but I guess we never took their flying abilities to heart, as we did those of birds. So, we studied how birds flew and a few intrepid and foolish experimenters even tried fixing feathered wings to their arms and jumping off cliffs, to tragic landings. But we did learn a lot about the principles of flight and aerodynamics, of lift and thrust and the astonishing contours of flight feathers that enabled birds to fly – and copied those for the wings we designed for our airplanes.

It's thought that feathers first evolved as insulation (and down feathers are still used for that by birds and ourselves). Then it was discovered that they could help the ancestors of birds on which they first appeared – smaller dinosaurs related to Tyrannosaurus Rex, believe it or not – to glide from branch to branch while escaping predators. From there flight evolved. And naturally, birds flew everywhere – exploring and colonizing every corner of the earth. They took on amazingly diverse shapes and sizes, lifestyles, diets, colours and methods of courting.

So much so, that on the heftier side of things we have the ostrich of Africa, standing 2 metres tall, unable to fly but able to run (in that lovely pansy manner!) at 70 kmph, and with a kick that can put out a lion's lights. Ostriches raise their broods communally, with the papas incubating perhaps a dozen eggs on the ground, and they will swallow just about anything.

At the other end of the scale is the iridescent blue bee hummingbird of Cuba and the Caribbean. The ladies, weightier than the gentlemen, tip the scales at just over 2.5 grams. Hummingbirds fly more like insects than conventional birds and will blur their wings at between 80 and 200 times per second, visiting perhaps 1,500 flowers every day for nectar in order to get the energy they require for their manic metabolism. They can fly in any direction they want, up and down, and even in reverse, their wingbeats generating lift and thrust on both the upstroke and downstroke, unlike other birds who only use the downstroke for this purpose. They can touch 48 kmph, and like others of their kind, go into a kind of torpor at night to save energy.

Waddlers, Waders, Wanderers and Wedded Wonders

And birds have settled everywhere: emperor penguins, so well insulated in their fur coats, nestle their tiny babies on their feet and embark on heroic fishing trips (usually one parent at a time) in the Southern Ocean. On land penguins waddle and hop hilariously; their wings have turned into flippers and are used for swimming, diving and smacking one another during territorial battles, making them look as if they are taking part in some slapstick Charlie Chaplin comedy! During blizzards they will huddle in great round flocks, with the outer members in the group gradually moving inwards so that they can warm up after being exposed to the direct ferocity of the icy winds.

The oceans and seas provide food and shelter for a plethora of species, from graceful terns to the wonderful romantic wandering albatrosses. These magnificent birds, with their 3.5-metre wingspans, scour the Southern Ocean, clocking over 120,000 kilometres per year. They glide low over the waves, using air currents caused by them to remain aloft, with the minimum expenditure of energy (nary a wingbeat!), and spend most of their lives on the wing, hunting fish. When gorged, some find it difficult to take off from the water again!

One of my favourite water birds are pelicans, whose bills can actually hold more than their bellies, but some of whose feeding habits can be

pretty ruthless, involving the scooping up of other birds and fish into their huge shopping-bag-like bills and gulping them down. Flotillas of pelicans may also encircle fish, harrying them towards the shore where they can be scooped up easily.

So don't get taken in by their small twinkling eyes and the absurd little crests they wear! But they look magnificent while soaring.

And then there are shorebirds: usually salt and pepper coloured species, with bills and legs of varying lengths depending on their preferred food preferences — they hunt around in the mud, on beaches or edges of water bodies. In their breeding season, some of them, like the ruffs, can bedeck themselves like noblemen in the court of Louis XVI, with ruffs and riffles adorning their necks. I often wonder if those court noblemen took fashion cues from these birds!

The bill-tips of shorebirds are acutely sensitive, as they probe blindly in the mud for worms, mollusks and other tasty titbits beneath the surface. Many shorebirds are migratory, and fly enormous distances over open oceans every autumn and spring. A bar-tailed godwit was recorded flying 13,560 kilometres non-stop in eleven days from Alaska to Tasmania! (A hatchback, averaging 20 kilometres per litre, would need a fuel tank that could hold 678 litres to cover this distance.) The celebrated Arctic tern clocks 25,000 kilometres between the Arctic and Antarctic on its annual migration.

With their wacky quacks and tail-wagging waddles, ducks and geese have fascinated us for eons and found a redolent place on many a dining table the world over. Again, many species are migratory; in India most are, flying in from Siberia, China and Central Asia to spend the balmy winters on the waterbodies, jheels, lakes and rivers in our subcontinent. They come in an astonishing variety of finery, from the handsome saffron-headed red-crested pochards (with their bundh-galla suits, flaming ginger heads and lurid pink bills), to the dazzling Mandarin duck of China (not a visitor here, sorry to say!). They too are masters of the skies; bar-headed geese have been spotted flying over Mount Everest, at an altitude where oxygen is virtually non-existent and temperatures are way below freezing. Now that's what you would call having superlative lung-power. (Birds have a respiratory system which allows the continuous passage of oxygen through their bloodstream, independent of whether they are inhaling or exhaling.)

Long-legged cranes (usually ashy-grey, white, black and with bits of red on their heads) have moved and inspired people all around the world. These tall, graceful birds have made a name for themselves through their evocative, elaborate courting dances, accompanied by much lovelorn trumpeting and bugling, not to mention prancing and wing-flapping. What's moved us most about them is their legendary fidelity: our own Sarus crane (the tallest flying bird in the world) is known to pine to death when its partner dies and so is protected by farmers in whose fields they hunt frogs, reptiles, fish, insects, aquatic plants and tubers and seeds. The red-faced, snow-white Siberian or great white crane, once a regular visitor to the Keoladeo National Park, no longer shows up; this particular flock of birds has been shot, trapped or poisoned to extinction while on its migratory flight over Afghanistan and Pakistan, from its breeding grounds in China. Another crane in trouble is the black-necked crane that breeds in the Tibetan Plateau and remote areas in Bhutan and Northeast India; though protected by Buddhist tradition, it is being seriously threatened by large packs of ferocious feral mastiffs in Ladakh.

Jungle Gems

Skulking around in the tangled, verdant depths of tropical jungles, especially in our region of the world, are a family of true dazzlers: the pheasants. Our peacock is just one among them; others include the gorgeous golden pheasant and Lady Amherst's pheasant from China and Myanmar, and the dazzling monal from the Himalayas. The most famous of course is our red jungle fowl, the progenitor of all our broilers and capons and tandoori chickens! Other pheasants too are good eating, and in the west (including the United Kingdom) are bred specially for annual shoots, in which even the allegedly animal-loving British royal family take enthusiastic part.

From the tropical jungles of Southeast Asia of Indonesia and Borneo come perhaps the most fanciful of all birds that stunned explorers like Alfred Russell Wallace: the fabulous birds of paradise. Elaborately attired in plumes, satiny finery and astonishing tails, they were ruthlessly hunted by tribals and locals for their plumes, till many species teetered on the brink of extinction. I saw some of these splendid birds in Singapore's Jurong Bird Park, and was truly gobsmacked. We humans really are a very envious and wanting species – and so have been plucking these (and so many other) birds of their finery to decorate ourselves! And unwittingly, we say we have 'a feather in our cap' when we achieve a personal milestone, admitting to their superiority!

Parrots 'R' Us

Parrots and parakeets (which are smaller and sleeker) around the world have captivated us like few other species. With their remarkable ability to mimic, parrots are thought to be (along with crows and other corvids) the brainiest of all birds. A fierce debate still rages over whether parrots – like the African grey – actually know what they're saying, or are simply mimicking us meaninglessly. One scientist has claimed that if we were to be birds, we would be parrots! Another mimicker par excellence is Australia's lyrebird, which can mimic everything thing from a chainsaw to a camera shutter perfectly. How their brains take in the information, process it and then enable the vocal cords to reproduce it perfectly is still not completely known.

GPS Superstars

Another family that has beguiled us for centuries are pigeons and doves. How do pigeons find their way back home to their dovecotes after being released from locations hundreds of miles away? Well, the same question could be asked of all those migratory species that turn up at a particular water body, or even garden, year after year – and nearly on the same date every year. Several hypotheses have been proposed to explain the phenomenon: it's now been generally accepted that birds use the Earth's magnetic field as a compass (apart from taking cues from geographic features such as river courses, coastlines, mountain ranges and now even our highways) and some astonishing explanations are being provided and being fiercely debated. It is now being proposed that migratory songbirds may actually be able to see the Earth's magnetic field, perhaps imprinted over what they are normally seeing, like an overlaying image, perhaps. Exactly how they visualize it remains to be discovered, but this is how the thinking goes!

The Singers Sing Their Songs

Songbirds form an enormous group of small birds, many migratory, many not. These are also calling passerines or perching birds and include around 5,000 species. Their specially developed voice-boxes (called syrinxes), enable them to whistle and warble so tunefully that we've kept many species caged (like canaries, mynas and shamas), so that they can sing for us and lift our spirts, especially on Monday mornings! Well, birds don't sing for us – they do it for each other. Usually, it is the gentlemen that sing in order to claim territory and attract the ladies. The ladies appear to like more elaborate and sometimes louder compositions because they indicate that the singer is in fine fettle and will give her babies strong genes.

And some songs can be truly wonderful: wander out onto a field in February and you may hear a tinkling waterfall of musical notes descending from the heavens. Look up and you may spot a tiny brown blurry speck circling around, its throat vibrating. A skylark. The song goes on for as long as five to ten minutes nonstop, then there's silence and the bird parachutes to the earth, vanishing amidst the clods, only to spring up again moments later to repeat the performance. Now try to sing in tune and run up several flights of stairs at the same time and you'll realize what this little bird is capable of. In India, one of our most renowned songsters is the white-rumped shama, a cousin of the familiar tuxedoed magpie-robin common in most gardens and also a virtuoso. Salim Ali picked the grey-winged blackbird as his favourite; as for myself, I never tire of listening to the recordings of the blue-whistling thrush I made while on a holiday to the hills.

Raptor!

No family of birds has impressed us more than the raptors: those magnificent birds of prey. Formidably armed with grappling iron talons, cruelly sharp hooked bills, incredible eyesight and powerful wings, they are fierce hunters of the skies, swooping down on unsuspecting victims – usually other birds and animals as large as foxes. Superpowers like the United States and the erstwhile Soviet Union used them as national emblems (the bald eagle is the national bird of the United States) as did conquerors like Julius Caesar and his Roman legions. The golden eagle is perhaps one of the most magnificent, a powerful hunter of the mountains capable of snatching up a fox or lamb with ease. The harpy eagle of the Amazon picks up monkeys and sloths from the treetops and is not a bird to be trifled with, what with its bear-like talons and razor-sharp bill.

Raptors come in a range of sizes, appetites and abilities. The magnificent peregrine falcon is the fastest living creature on earth, clocking up to 320 kmph as it stoops upon some unfortunate pigeon, its wings folded tight along its body, a streaking aerodynamic arrowhead. (We're designing stealth jets with the same profile.) Hawks like our shikra (a species of sparrowhawk) dodge deftly through branches and creepers in tangled jungles and woods as they streak and swerve towards their prey — small birds and animals like squirrels.

Other raptors like vultures and kites are content to scavenge and clean up the leftovers of animal kills — and now the rubbish and offal we throw about everywhere so generously. Our black kite is a familiar sight in our skies — especially over cities — and it's well worth watching them fly. They will corkscrew down after a dead rat in the road, snatch it up neatly right under your front bumper and spiral upwards triumphantly with it before you even fully realize what's happening! They bank and turn with the merest flick of tail and wings, a lesson in maximizing the use air currents and breeze and minimizing the expenditure of energy.

Vultures, alas, have never been too popular because of what we think are their repulsive, filthy dining habits. They will plunge their ugly naked heads and necks deep into a festering carcass and gobble and grab what meat has still been left on the bones, fighting each other beak and claw as they do so. In reality, they are among the cleanest birds around: their heads and beaks are naked so that festering flesh doesn't stick to them and spread infection, and they are very particular about their personal hygiene for this reason too. It has been said that a flock of 200 vultures can clean up the carcass of a buffalo in around half an hour. As a scavenging service they are invaluable: cleaning up roadkill and the carcasses of dead animals before bacteria could spread, causing disease. And yes, they have strong stomachs: the bearded vulture or lammergeier that circles the heavens above the mountains picks up the bones of dead animals and drops them from great heights. The bones shatter on rocks below and the birds swoop down for the nutritious marrow exposed by the splintered bones. They may even swallow the bones whole and it's said that the bones begin to dissolve as soon as they enter the stomach, even before the entire bone finds its way in.

Sadly, vultures had one huge Achillies heel: their inability to deal with an analgesic that was widely given to livestock — diclofenac (which even we use). Traces of this drug, which remained in the carcasses of buffaloes which vultures consumed, were enough to destroy their kidneys and kill the birds. India lost more than 95 per cent of her vultures due to this and even now various once-common species, like the long-billed and white-rumped vulture, are critically endangered. It just shows how careful we need to be about such matters like introducing new drugs, fertilizers and pesticides into our environment.

Night of the Hunters

Owls have taken over the night shift. With their huge forward-facing eyes, asymmetrical ears and soundproof plumage, they are a nightmare for rodents such as rats. The barn owl, found virtually all over the world, with its heart-shaped face, beautiful mushroom plumage and blood-curdling shrieks, is a specialist rat-

hunter. Its disc-shaped face works like a satellite dish, focusing sound to its ears, and its wings have fuzzy edges so that they remain completely silent as the owl whooshes down on its unsuspecting victim. At a raptor rescue centre in America, I watched with disbelief as four barn owls, recovering from injuries, flew towards me across their large aviary in absolute silence. I could only thank my stars I wasn't a rat. Barn owls account for a huge population of rats — and rats as we

127

know account for 20 per cent of our foodgrain stocks — so the birds' contribution is invaluable.

Owls too come in various sizes and specialties, from the tiny pygmy owl to the enormous eagle-owls which can easily take down a peacock. One of the commonest in India is the dumpy spotted owlet, brown with icing-sugar-like spots on its head and a truly endearing manner. They may huddle in pairs outside their hollows early in the morning, often passionately kissing each other and preening, before they retire for the day.

Little Brown Jobs

The tiny-tot warblers, in their myriad combinations of brown, beige, tan, biscuit, grey, white and olive green (dubbed 'little brown jobs') often drive birders nuts — because they can be so difficult to identify. Most (like our tailorbird and the plain prinia) have voices ten times their size: I call them Bose-speaker birds, and often it is only through their calls and songs that they can be identified. Some of these are migratory and though weighing perhaps under 10 grams may fly thousands of kilometres every autumn to spend the forthcoming winter in warmer lands — like our subcontinent.

Homebodies

All birds build nests in which they bring up their young: some, like the big eagles, build huge twiggy edifices high up in the canopy, which they embellish year on year; others are content with a scrape in the ground, and yet others, like our famous baya weaver, craft and weave beautiful retort-shaped nests out of grass and straw. Watch a weaver at work and you are watching a true craftsman going about his task. Of course, this is all done to impress the ladies and sometimes if either the master weaver himself is not happy, or the lady finds that the home she has been invited to has no central air conditioning, he may in a fit of pique destroy the nest and start over. But he is one wily son of a gun: if the lady is happy with the home she has been offered, he settles her in on her eggs, and then commences on another nest in order to woo yet another lady, and then maybe a third!

Canny, Cunning and Very Clever

Crows may not be the most popular of birds, but hands down they are among the most intelligent. They have solved puzzles, opened locks and worked out problems logically in a manner that has left scientists scratching their heads in amazement. They have face-recognition abilities too: make friends with a crow and it will remember you; aim a catapult at it and it will not forget this either, and buzz you mercilessly every time it sees you — calling up a backup gang of friends for good measure. Crows have long memories and are not very forgiving. They are also known to have a sense of humour: so many times, I've watched a twinkle-eyed mischief-maker cheekily tug at the train of a peacock, just for the heck of it. And I know it's just doing it to pull down the strutting VIP bird a notch or two — and every time it's made me smile. Crows (along with their relatives, the magpies) have a thing for bling and will pick up shiny trinkets whenever they can, often decorating their untidy nests with these. (One crow famously made its nest entirely out of spectacle frames it had purloined from a local optician's outlet!) And crows, like so many other birds, clearly enjoy flying for the sake of flying. I've watched jungle crows fly towards sheer mountain slopes, and ride steeply upwards on the updrafts produced as the wind hits the mountains. Then nearly breasting the ridge-tops they dive down, down, down towards the valley floor before levelling out and repeating the performance again and again, hoarsely cawing with sheer glee and exultation.

Trouble in the Skies

Like most other living creatures in the world, many species (460, according to the IUCN) of birds are threatened, endangered or perilously close to extinction. In India the list runs to 182 species that are in trouble. Several species have gone extinct: in India, for example, the pink-headed duck and probably soon-to-be, the Great Indian Bustard. The Siberian crane no longer spends its winters in Bharatpur. And we know the fate that befell the vultures. The dodo from Mauritius is perhaps the most well-known of birds to have gone extinct, and entirely due to us.

We must never underestimate the threat we pose to birds or for that matter any living creature, whether due to climate change, global warming or any other reason linked or not linked to it. In America, the population of the endemic passenger pigeon was estimated at up to 5 billion birds in the nineteenth century, and they were hunted for food by the native Americans. With the arrival of the white man in America, the hunting went nuclear, and the last wild passenger pigeon was shot in 1900. The last captive passenger pigeon, 'Martha', died in the Cincinnati Zoo on 1 September 1914.

The importance of birds in keeping our potpourri planet in good health (and us, in good spirits) cannot be underestimated. For example, they are vital for seed dispersal and forest regeneration. Birds like hornbills, barbets and mynas eat figs, drupes and berries and scatter their seeds in their droppings far and wide, enabling new growth. Even wastrel feeders like parakeets, who may drop more fruit than they consume, are useful: deer and antelope often hang around beneath trees that they inhabit, waiting for the dropped fruit, consume it and in turn wander around and spread the seeds in their droppings. Birds are also responsible for pollination; sunbirds, hummingbirds, warblers (of myriad kinds), mynas et al. help themselves to flowers and nectar and, in doing so, pollinate the plants. (The jungle myna, for example, has a 'brush' on its forehead with which it picks up pollen!)

As pest controllers birds are invaluable, keeping the population of insect pests under control. Millions of ravenous baby birds are fed an unending supply of caterpillars, grubs, larvae and insects by their parents (who may well be vegetarian!) because

131

of the high protein they contain, and which, if allowed to feed or metamorphosize, could defoliate entire forests. Red-whiskered bulbul parents nesting in a bougainvillea creeper outside my bedroom would fetch insects or caterpillars every ten minutes or so through the day, to stuff the faces of their forever hungry brood of three. Rosy starlings produce baby-booms when the population of locusts periodically explodes, keeping their numbers below gargantuan proportions. Owls, as we have seen, keep the number of rodents such as rats in check. Scavengers clean up the festering remains of kills and now help us keep our roads clean as they pick up roadkill. Some birds in fact have changed their food habits and preferences: gulls, egrets and storks — like the adjutants — who were once fishers, now flock to garbage dumps and city promenades: gulls in fact, especially in the west, even boldly mug city-dwellers of their fish and chips and other snacks.

Climate change and global warming have affected ecosystems and life directly and indirectly all over the world, and birds are no exception. The mass felling of especially tropical rainforests has not only contributed to global warming but caused habitat destruction on a grand scale, which directly impacts every living creature living in those habitats, birds included. It has also caused us to change our crop patterns: because of changed weather patterns, we may stop planting one crop in favour of another, and this in turn affects birds who depended on the insects that fed off those original crops. Sharply rising temperatures have caused frighteningly humungous wildfires, burning everything in their path to cinders. Climate extremes and unpredictable weather patterns can play havoc with the natural timetables upon which birds base their lives. For example, bee-eaters and kingfishers nest in holes they excavate on the sandy banks of rivers and water-courses in summer, well before the rains. Their babies must be out of their homes and fending for themselves before the rains hit and the rivers rise. A single ill-timed cloudburst (more likely now than ever before) that causes the river to rage and rise and undermines the sandbanks can wash away an entire brand-new brood of birds. And with the climate changing so fast and so drastically, the chances of this happening are only increasing. The early melting of sea ice has doomed breeding populations of emperor penguins as their babies drown en masse, their woolly-coats not yet waterproof.

Climate change in the form of failed monsoons causes drought: with foliage drying up, insects may not breed, in turn curtailing the breeding of birds whose babies depend on those insects. Birds have to keep their breeding in tune with the arrival of insects and caterpillars and many find it hard to do so when the climate changes so frequently and radically. This 'mismatch' has led to situations when, for example, birds who find it difficult to adjust their timetables quickly enough hatch their young after a caterpillar-boom is over, meaning there is less to go around for the new generation of fledglings.

Climate change has also caused changes in migratory timetables. Birds that breed in the northern hemisphere, in summer, may leave for their migratory winter haunts later, as the summers get longer in the north. Also, in summer they may have to fly even further north to find suitable breeding sites as the heat builds up in their original territories, and there is a limit to how far north they can eventually go! For countries like India that may mean we see late arrivals and perhaps early departures. Birds that live in the foothills of the mountains may have to move to higher altitudes as the weather gets warmer, and here again, they may eventually run out of altitude!

Many species are not bothered as much with temperatures: they time their departures and arrivals depending on the length of the day, and this remains constant year on year. Come rain or shine they will set off on their epic journeys on virtually the same date every year, and this could prove to be disastrous. Most migrants to India arrive in the balmy winter months, the bulk arriving by October and November. If India is experiencing a heatwave in any of those months, or an unexpected monsoon deluge, due to climate change, many long-distance migrants may find themselves in conditions not as salubrious as they expected and suffer. It's something like you turning up at a holiday resort, equipped with sunscreen, shades and swimsuit, only to find that it's pouring nonstop and you haven't brought any rain gear!

Storms and hurricanes caused by climate change will naturally also affect birds: migratory birds may be blown off course (if not killed directly), especially over the open oceans, and resident species may have their homes destroyed as trees come down and bushes are blown to shreds.

Research on how climate change and global warming effect birds is still nascent, and here the role of ordinary birders is proving to be invaluable. They report the comings and goings of species to monitoring platforms which can then figure out shifting population trends and the possible reasons for these, over a period of time, leading us to a better understanding of what's happening. I for one keep wondering about the disappearance of several species that I used to regularly see in my neck of the woods. The common babbler has vanished, I hardly get to see the delightful brahminy starling anymore and the lovely plum-headed parakeets no long streak through the skies over the house, whistling like schoolboys as they once used to. Where have they gone, and why have they gone? The non-availability of a favourite food could be one reason. Could that be in any way linked to the changes in climate we have been experiencing — directly or indirectly? The chirpy house sparrow has also gone (not from all of Delhi though), and several reasons have been cited for its disappearance: one of them is that our houses are not as open and hospitable to them as before. We've enclosed all our balconies and verandas and sealed up our apartments for air conditioning, as global warming has made the summers so much hotter and intolerable.

Birds play an as important role in the upkeep of our potpourri planet, as every other living creature. And they have one advantage over many others: you may see a tiger or spot a whale, if you are lucky, once or twice in your lifetime, and be wowed. But you can see and enjoy the company of birds every single day, almost no matter where you live, be it city, suburb, country or hill station. To let them vanish will be like obliterating something essential from our very spirit, and we can't have that, can we?

CHAPTER 8: WARM-BLOODED WONDERS — MAMMALS

Of all living creatures on our planet, we associate most closely with mammals, because we are mammals too. We can regulate our body temperature and keep it constant; we give birth to live young (with a few exceptions that lay eggs); we suckle our babies and bestow a lot of TLC on them and educate them for long periods of time (some parents would say 'forever'!). And we have the best brains in the business, even though, despite being aware of global warming and climate change (climate tantrums, actually) we don't seem to be using them very much or very wisely.

And many of the over 6,500 species of mammals that share our potpourri planet with us have skillsets which we can only envy, some of which we are trying to bio-engineer or reverse-engineer for our own benefit. Sadly since 1500, some 76 mammal species have gone extinct and today some 1,141 species are threatened with extinction. Apart from their special skillsets, mammals play as vital a role in the maintenance of life on our planet as do all the other groups of living creatures. Sitting on the top of the woodpile, as it were, are the big carnivores — and ourselves, of course — apex (and as we are, reckless and greedy) predators in the food chain and in charge of the whole business of the circle of life. It may not seem like the end of the world if one mammal or any other species goes extinct, but we may really not have any idea of the enormity of the loss because some of the skillsets these creatures possess are truly remarkable and can teach us much more than just how truly astonishing and wonderful life on earth is.

Weird Is Wonderful

Let's start with one of the weirdest mammals on the planet: Australia's duck-billed platypus, now ranked as a threatened species by IUCN's Red List of Threatened Species. When European naturalists first saw the body of the platypus back in 1799, they were convinced they were being had: they suspected it to be parts of various different animals that had been sewn up together. Here was a mammal that laid eggs, had a 'beak' like a duck, a tail like a beaver, feet like an otter, armed (the gentlemen) with a venomous spur on its tail. And that is not all: that wacky duckbill is equipped with something like 500,000 electrical sensors, and the platypus hunts for food (crayfish, worms, insect larvae) by diving into the murky depths, closing its eyes and ears and using its bill like a metal detector, sweeping it from side to side to pick up electrical pulses given out by its meals.

Staying on in Australia (which has more than its fair share of weirdos!) is the cute, cuddly koala. With their button eyes and cute, tubby, fluffy bodies, koalas sleep twenty hours a day and subsist on a diet of eucalyptus leaves, which are not very nutritious and too toxic for other herbivores to stomach. This cuddly little creature has a loud bellow (to woo mates and warn off others) and can also be a ferocious fighter. It is threatened, with destruction of habitat being one major issue, especially wildfires, which in this age of climate change have become far too frequent and ferocious for comfort. Heart-rending pictures of fur-singed koalas, clinging on to the charred remains of their favourite eucalyptus tree after a fire, have appeared in the press, underlying the huge distress these animals have been put through.

No question, Australia is best known for its kangaroos — easily the champion kick-boxer marsupial of them all! Apart from its unique appearance and those massive thunder-thighs and enormous feet, with which it hops at up to 70 kmph, the kangaroo has other astonishing USPs. What's interesting scientists now is that despite having a diet similar to that of livestock, kangaroos do not emit large quantities of digestive methane via burping, exhaling and farting! Hydrogen, which is a byproduct of fermentation, is instead converted into acetate and used to boost energy with the help of bacteria. Scientists are now toying with the idea of using that same bacteria in cattle and sheep so that they stop burping and farting methane, and contributing to global warming! (Methane is twenty-three times a more dangerous greenhouse gas criminal than carbon dioxide!)

But what endears me most to kangaroos is the sheer, dogged survival spirit of their babies, called joeys. When they are born after a gestation period of just over a month, they are the size of a lima bean, and now must climb what the joey equivalent

of a thickly forested Mt Everest must be, through their mother's thick fur, in search of a teat. At this time, the tiny joey uses its forelimbs — its hindlegs are mere stubs. Once it finds a teat in its mother's pouch, it will hold on and not let go. Here, safe and snug, it will stay till about nine months old. It just shows that no matter how tiny and vulnerable you may seem, if you have the fighting spirit to survive, you can, no matter how great the odds. Now and in the future, we are going to need that fighting spirit like never before!

Pangolin Problems

Mammals come in a bewildering variety of shapes and sizes, and one of the strangest must be the pangolin. With its wonderfully scaly body (the scales are made of that wonder substance keratin) the Indian pangolin is seriously threatened with extinction, the leading cause being poaching. In our eternal wisdom, we have decided that its scales have aphrodisiacal and medicinal qualities and have poached the poor animal to the point of extinction. Other causes for its decline are deforestation and habitat destruction, which again causes, and is a result of, climate change. But seriously, we first have to understand that pangolin scales will not make us any more macho or virile, but instead make us look stupider than we already are!

Batting for Bats

Bats must be among the least popular, most misunderstood and useful mammals on the planet. They are the only mammals capable of true flight, and may fly more agilely than birds. Their wings are formed by membranes stretched between the equivalent of their fingers. Ah, you might say, but they are so hideously ugly, what with their smashed rats' faces and evil little eyes. And boy, do they stink. Bat fug in a cave can make you faint! Besides they harbour malevolent viruses like rabies and may even have been responsible for Covid-19! Worse, like Dracula, some drink blood! So, what's there to like?

For a start, their dung makes excellent fertilizer and is harvested for that. They are pest-controllers par excellence – a single small brown bat can account for 1,000 mosquitoes per hour. They are great pollinators and seed dispersers: bananas, mangoes, figs and agave, for example, are beholden to them for this, not to mention ourselves. And they have among the most sophisticated hunting techniques in the animal kingdom, using ultrasonic echolocation to locate, target and home in on their swiftly and very erratically moving prey in pitch darkness. They send out a stream of high-pitched ultrasonic squeaks and wait for the echoes to bounce off their victim back to them, calculating size, shape, speed and direction in milliseconds as they zero in on their target. We are only now beginning to appreciate the astonishing complexity involved in this process and how bats overcome some of the seemingly intractable challenges in their path, all at breakneck speed.

It is thought that global warming may cause higher mortality among some species of bats, especially those with a low reproductive rate, leading to a possible population crash and extinction. Fruit bats may migrate to less warm habitats to which they are not accustomed. Three species within the genus Leptonycteris are critical to the pollination of the blue agave, from which tequila is made, and their extinction would be disastrous for the industry! Certainly the extinction of say an insectivorous or pollinating species of bat does not augur well for the health of the planet.

All in the Family: Primates

From bats, we move to baboons and their ilk – the primates. From brilliant little problem-solving capuchins to war-mongering chimpanzees, primates (and especially apes) have fascinated us for very obvious reasons. (Stand outside the monkeys' cages in a zoo, and you'll know exactly why!) With their intelligence, agility and ability to adapt they have spread around the world, from South America and Africa to Southeast Asia. Now some species — like the langurs and macaques — are quite happy to settle in cities like New Delhi and Jaipur, where unfortunately, they make a nuisance of themselves, though the fault as usual is more ours than theirs. The great apes perhaps have been of the most interesting for us — gorillas, chimpanzees and orangutans — ever since Darwin stipulated that they were our ultimate grandparents and so deserved some respect! And we've used monkeys and chimps for some pretty radical (and ethically questionable) experiments: medical and social. Anyone who has ever popped a pill owes a debt of gratitude to the poor chimp on which it was first tested, being given doses that ultimately killed it.

Wholesale deforestation — which leads to climate change — has affected great ape populations radically and more directly. The clearing of Indonesia's tropical rainforests for palm-oil plantations have left the gentle-eyed orangutan high and dry, literally teetering on the brink of extinction. Gorilla and chimpanzee habitats in Africa have been cleared for agriculture; besides, civil wars in some regions have played havoc with habitats and certainly their peace of mind. And yet each of these three — the chimpanzee, gorilla and orangutan — have taught us one lesson regarding the power of a single person to change things for the better: Jane Goodall did it for the chimps, the late Dian Fossey for the gorillas and Biruté Galdikas for the orangutans.

The golden lion tamarin (also known as the golden marmoset), native to the jungles of Eastern Brazil, was critically endangered due to deforestation, fragmentation, hunting and the pet trade. Captive-breeding programmes in several zoos around the world (including Gerald Durrell's zoo in Jersey) helped in making the populations recover somewhat, but this high-spirited, beautiful little monkey is still not quite out of the woods in the wild.

Are Rats, Us?

Rodents are not everyone's favourite animal group. Squirrels are perhaps one member of the group that might be the exception. Apart from their eloquent eyes, bushy tails and endearing way of sitting up and holding nuts in their 'hands' while delicately nibbling them (like socialites at a cocktail party partaking of canapes), squirrels have phenomenal memories. Before winter they stock up on nuts and acorns, burying them in thousands of little holes they dig in the ground – while being ever watchful that they're not being spied upon by their compatriots. When winter arrives, they harvest these buried nuts, but will invariably forget the location of some, which in the following spring will sprout – the squirrel equivalent of tree plantation!

Up in Alaska scientists have been studying the effects of global warming on the hibernating habits of Alaskan ground squirrels. They may hibernate for over six months in winter, with the gentlemen awakening some ten or fifteen days before the ladies, to enable their testosterone levels to rise enough to make them rakish macho dudes, raring to welcome the ladies. With global warming, it has been found that while the gents still awake at the same time, the ladies are becoming earlier risers and pop out of their burrows while the gents are still gearing up to become all virile and manly (and may still be in their pyjamas and with six-months-worth of halitosis), something, alas, the ladies would not be impressed by at all. This in the long run could lead to a decline in population – and in extreme cases, extinction.

On the other hand, a study on North American red squirrels has shown that they may be undergoing genetic alteration in response to climate change. Female squirrels are now giving birth around eighteen days earlier than normal, because the squirrels' staple food, spruce cones, are now available earlier (due to climate change). But a part of this change is also being caused by natural selection, and those ladies who were genetically inclined to breed earlier will thrive. In a nutshell, the life-cycles of plants and animals are changing due to global warming, and those that can swing with the changes and seek out new comfort zones will survive. Those that cannot will go extinct.

Like it or not, rats 'r' us! Scientists say we have similar psychologies. Put 500 rats in a one-foot-square box and see what happens. Do the same with people and exactly the same thing happens. And we've discovered that everything causes cancer in rats (at mind-boggling doses of the carcinogen, of course). We've grown a human ear on a rat's back using stem cells which were turned into cartilage cells which in turn, were placed in a plastic framework of tubes resembling a human ear. They are beady-eyed and scaly-tailed and like us, canny, cunning, and vicious. They have travelled the world on every mode of transport. And they (and their cousins, mice) are intelligent and curious: one little mouse that was a houseguest sat quietly on the sideboard, watching Ratatouille on TV with me with great interest! But ever since they spread the Bubonic plague via their fleas in Europe and Asia and killed off half the population, they have not been forgiven.

So how have rats dealt with climate change and global warming? Some scientists say actually very well, others, more conservative, say theoretically they could do very well, but that it is difficult to scientifically study them! Rats are fast-breeder reactors (a female can have as many as seventy-two babies a year!) and get especially frisky when it's warm; summer is when they really roll in the hay. In cities in the Northern Hemisphere – like New York (a great place for rats of all kinds) – they doss down in their burrows in winter: one, because it's too cold out and two, because there are less people around discarding half-eaten pizzas and burgers everywhere. But with winters getting warmer and shorter, they are now delighted to be able to romance and frolic (in uncompromising positions, as killjoys would say) in the balmier weather, slipping in a couple of more litters every year, leading to what some have called a ratpocalypse!

Flash floods in cities, such as the one faced by Delhi in 2023, caused by climate change may also lead to the population of rats to explode suddenly, as it leads to the breakdown of infrastructure, especially garbage collection, and thus more eat-all-you-can buffets for rats! Like politicians, they are the most adaptable of animals and so are quite likely to use climate change to their advantage.

Speaking of rats, we can't leave out the remarkable naked mole rat: one of the ugliest but most charming rodents around, that lives in East Africa. This is one creature that actually revels in lethal (for other rats and us) levels of carbon dioxide, is stubbornly cancer resistant, lives far longer than any of its ilk, virtually feels no pain and lives together in large family groups of up to 300 members in underground burrows and tunnels, ruled – like bees and termites are – by a single queen! You can imagine what a tizzy they've put scientists into. They certainly don't need to be unduly worried about high carbon dioxide emissions!

Big Boys in the Big Blues

We dive now into the deep oceans where the big guys – whales, dolphins and porpoises – live and hunt. Ocean temperatures are currently at their highest-ever levels (over 21 degrees Celsius), and this bodes ill for the future of these giants. It affects the availability and distribution of krill and plankton in the ocean, on which these giants depend. The unpredictable breaking up of the ice packs at the poles disturbs their undersea migratory routes, and the increased concentration of pollutants in the water, as a result of global warming and our activities, certainly cannot be good for their health. Microplastics in the milk of big mama whales may reach toxic levels, killing their suckling infants. Ocean currents shift and change as the waters warm and may confuse salmon heading back to the rivers where they were spawned – and are awaited by these giants. As the waters warm, these great animals – as well as fish – need to dive deeper, where the water is still cold, to find enough to eat, as cold water holds more nutrients.

We're still mining and probing the ocean beds for oil and minerals, opening up vast areas for oil exploration and possible extraction. This not only causes obvious pollution from spills, but also causes problems for whales and dolphins who communicate across vast distances with their repertoire of clicks and songs. The rumble of ships' engines and the blasting and dredging that goes on

makes the
ocean an
aurally inhospitable
environment. The
Ganges is being
dredged in
areas to
enable huge
barges and
tourist ships to ply,
causing distress to the highly
endangered Ganges
river dolphin, who is blind
and who depends nearly
entirely on sound (and
echolocation) to move
around and hunt in the
murky waters.

Fang and Claw and Terrifying Roar

Large carnivores too have been affected — to a lesser or greater degree — by climate change and global warming, though this is an area that needs more study. Among the most seriously affected of these is the seal-hunting polar bear: the early and large-scale melting of sea ice has made it so difficult for the bears to hunt seals that they've been reduced to taking sea birds' eggs and upturning garbage bins in towns. Snow leopards up in the high Himalayas are having to move higher up due to warming, and a similar fate has overtaken the rare Ethiopian wolf, which is now virtually running out of altitude. In the mountains, global warming has caused loss of permafrost, the retreating of glaciers and the evaporating of small water bodies, such as springs and streams, as well as the drying up of pastures on which the prey of snow leopards depended.

Changing weather patterns and extreme weather events, which are getting uncomfortably regular, affect the health and numbers of the prey species of many carnivores. Blazing wildfires across vast tracts of forests or grasslands are straightforward killers, both of prey and predator — and the plants the prey species depend upon.

Species like the leopard and wolf, being highly adaptable, may fare better in dealing with climate change, but these — and some of the other carnivores like tigers and lions — may well take the easy way out when their prey base diminishes: they go for livestock, which brings them into deadly confrontation with us.

Memory Bankers: Elephants

The same fate awaits the elephants, who wander enormous distances in search of water and fodder. India has an estimated 25, 000–30,000 elephants (a 20 per cent decline in population has been recorded in the last five years); Africa has over 400,000 elephants, but two countries – Namibia and Zimbabwe – have plans to cull herds. As they search for water and nutritious plants in increasingly drier and hotter landscapes, elephants come into conflict with us. Paddy fields, orchards, grain godowns and even the village bar and lounge (not to mention passing sugarcane-loaded trucks) make for easier, possibly tastier and certainly more entertaining options. That is until the firecrackers explode and flaming torches are hurled at them by infuriated villagers and farmers. Also, we have infringed upon and destroyed their ancient migratory routes with our tea, coffee and rice plantations, and they will not be deterred as they move through these ancient routes to their traditional feeding grounds.

As global warming and climate change affects ecosystems, habitats and the availability of food and water in those habitats, it will affect the lives of the animals that live in those habitats. Prolonged dry seasons, droughts, wildfires due to lightning strikes in dry grasslands or tinderbox forests (some insidiously started by us) or flash floods due to torrential downpours will have obviously disastrous consequences for the inhabitants of those areas. For many species of wildlife, global warming and climate change are increasingly making our once beautiful potpourri planet a very inhospitable place to live in and raise their young.

PART II

The Planet Today

"DO SOMETHING"

SELF REFLECT

I ♥ 🌍

CHAPTER 1: MAMA NATURE'S HISSY FITS: FLOODS, FIRE, FUMES, FURY AND FILTH

We could call them the nefarious five and they are now wreaking havoc in our once pristine sapphire planet. We ignored, abused, defied and defiled Mother Nature to such an extent and for so long, that she's now making it clear that she has had enough. She's striking back, and we're not liking it one bit.

Floods

In 2023, the message was delivered personally to me in Delhi, where I live. Cloudbursts in the mountains of the Himalayas not only caused havoc in those regions, but caused the mighty Yamuna to swell, about 2 kilometres away from my home, to such an extent that her waters were lapping at the gates of my residential complex in North Delhi. Several houses (and many cars) just down the road were drowned in filthy swirling and very angry waters. The Ring Road, which I use to get everywhere, turned into Ring River, flowing swiftly under the three magnificent old bridges built from across the Red Fort by the great Mughals, to access Salimgarh at a time when the river actually flowed along its great sandstone walls. The Yamuna had reclaimed her old bed.

As for me, there was disbelief that one's whole life could be turned upside down virtually without notice: I began to worry if there was enough water, food and medical supplies in the house, and hoping that the electricity and Wi-Fi would stay on. Houses down the road had no power for five days, because of the fear of 440 volts sizzling through the water. Our sainted politicians — some of whose very comfortable homes were also within lapping distance of the waters — could do no better than wag their pathetic fingers and shriek shrilly at one another. About a month after the floods, some of the over 20,000+ people who had had to be evacuated were still camped out in tents on the roadside, wondering what to do with their lives.

It was not difficult to figure out the chain of events (long-term and short-term), which led to this pretty pass. We've heated up the world, causing greater evaporation from the oceans, leading to the build of up of vast battalions of towering thunderheads, which just have to let go sooner rather than later. So they do, suddenly and unexpectedly, like a humungous water balloon in the sky bursting, usually over the mountains, causing dinky tinkling streams to turn into weapons of mass destruction as they hurtle down the slopes, taking down everything and every living thing in their path: boulders as big as apartment blocks, trees, holiday resorts, multi-storey buildings, bridges, sixteen-wheeler trucks, cars (like corks), buses, places of worship and even dams, sparing none. They can (and do) dump a year's rainfall in a few hours, and how does one prepare for that?

Frankly we asked for it. We built tottering teetering structures cheek by jowl right next to the banks of these streams and rivers; we blasted and tunnelled through the fragile mountains till they trembled and crumbled and came crashing down (remember the Himalayas are made of fragile stuff, like crushed shells, that was pushed up from the seabed) when saturated with water. We carved up the mountainsides for six-lane highways, we cut down the trees en masse so that they no longer stapled the fragile soil in place, we bottled up these swiftly flowing streams and rivers with scores of dams, backing up their waters and leaving them no choice but to have an aneurysm and burst their banks with pent-up pressure. Look at Shimla! Most of this once-lovely hill station has

been illegally built on slopes inclined at 45 to 60 degrees, some even as steep as 75 degrees, whereas the safe limit for building on mountain slopes is 30 degrees or less. Worse, one of the main transgressors of all building rules is the government itself, which framed those rules, and which is so quick to point fingers at everyone else. It looks dangerously like the entire hill station is about to topple into the valley and gorge below.

And down in the plains, where these rivers eventually broaden and flow, we built on and 'developed' the floodplains, so that there was nowhere for the excess water to swirl and deposit the silt, except into our houses, markets and roads. Of course, there are laws that prevent us from doing much of the above. But firstly, they're rarely implemented (this is a traditional, almost genetic affliction with us, because there are fortunes to be made by ignoring the rules), and secondly, we are now busily watering down those laws to

make it easier for us to carry on in this bindass kamikaze manner. It's really like letting a hyped-up seventeen-year-old get behind the wheel of a Formula 1 racing car after a night of hitting the bars.

Aiding and Abetting

Here is an example of how, so to say, we legally added water to the milk: way back in 1927 the Indian Forests Act marked out areas which were defined as forests. Decades later, in October 1980, the Forest Conservation Act came into being and laid down that all the areas that were defined as forests in the earlier act be protected from 'non-forest' activities. Thus, you could not cut down trees, mine, build and so on in these places unless you had the permission of the Central Government. The 1980 law had been winked at wholesale, especially after 1991, and land use had been usually allowed for almost every activity – ironically, except agriculture! Also, there were huge tracts of forests in the country which had not been included in the original demarcation and were thus open to total exploitation. In 1996, a gentleman by the name of Godavarman Thirumulpad, concerned about what was happening in the Nilgiris, raised this issue in the Supreme Court. In a landmark judgement, the Supreme Court held that all areas that fitted the dictionary meaning of the word 'forest' were to be taken into account, not just those officially recorded by the earlier Forest Conservation Act, regardless of who owned them. It asked states to identify these so far 'unofficial' forests and accord them due protection. Some states did, others, like Haryana, were very reluctant to comply. Till 2015, around 180,000 acres of the Aravallis in Gurugram and Faridabad was classified as 'yet to be decided', and so no protection was accorded to this area, opening it up to gross abuse.

But the 'development' lobby and big industrialists did not like this new definition of forests at all. Worse (for them), in 2006, the Forests Rights Act was passed, which declared that 'local stakeholders' – communities that lived in and depended on the forests – held the rights to those forests and had to agree to any change in land use that was being contemplated. Again, hurdles were put in the way: officials were slow to identify forests that villagers held rights to and notify the government. But then, in 2013, villagers got together and managed to stop a bauxite mining project in their village in Orissa. They went to the Supreme Court, which sided with them and the project was shelved.

After this, since 2014, 'development' lobbies in the government and outside began a campaign maintaining that all this was resulting in 'delays in issuing clearances', and so by inference, holding back the country's economic development. In 2023, the government, passed – without any discussion or debate, which is the democratic way to go about such things – a bill amending the Forest Conservation Act. What they did was to go back to the earlier, pre-1996 definition of forests, in essence bulldozing over the Supreme Court's verdict, and held that henceforth only areas earlier officially recorded as forests would come under the protection of the act. In other forested areas, you could do pretty much as you pleased. They also held that no environment clearances would be required for any project within 100 kilometres of our international borders, ostensibly for the security of the nation. Most of our border areas are either fragile desert ecosystems or amongst the richest in biodiversity, as in the northeastern states. Conservationists and ecologists say that the losses we will incur due to habitat destruction and change in land use in these areas will be far greater than any gains to national security. Such changes, they say, can lead to internal strife – as locals affected by such activities are not going to be happy – which can be more dangerous and divisive than external strife. (What struck me was that during the Vietnam war, the Vietcong won because they used their thick, steamy, malaria-ridden tropical jungles for cover, which so frustrated the Americans that they used that notorious defoliant 'Agent Orange' to clear the jungles – in spite of which, they lost the war!) I would also imagine that it would be far more difficult for an enemy to hack through impenetrable, mosquito- and leech-ridden tropical rainforests and swamps, than to rumble down wide smooth roads that have been built in their place.

The Forest Survey of India fears that 28 per cent of India's forests could be put at risk if this bill were to become a law – which it now has. What can now go on in these 'demoted' forest areas? They can be turned into plantations (profit-making but not good for ecosystems) and even used for tourism – turned into zoos and safari parks (already they're thinking of vast safari parks stocked with hippos et al. in the Aravallis!) Now, 'compensatory afforestation' can be done anywhere: there's the huge 75,000 crore Great Nicobar Development Plan being plotted in the pristine Nicobar Islands, which are replete with endemic species. This will include a container transshipment terminal, an international airport and two new coastal cities, and is said to have 'geostrategic' importance for defence. Some 94 lakh trees have been condemned to die, but never mind — trees are to be planted in dust-blown Haryana to compensate for the loss. (Tell that to the Nicobar megapode and Nicobar sparrowhawk among others — maybe they would like to fly over and settle in a Gurugram gated colony!)

Only 21 per cent of India's land area has forest cover, of which 12.37 per cent is intact forest. The target is 33 per cent of intact forest. But with the government adopting this attitude, were aren't likely to achieve it anytime soon, and more disasters seem to be in the offing: avalanches, cloudbursts and haywire weather that upsets cropping patterns and harvests, and with it everyone's lives.

Our first (usually official) response to such disasters is always a po-faced denial: oh no, we were not responsible for what happened, it was just nature's fury, and what can you do about that? An act of God, God's will. And we forget it very quickly, so will face the same crisis sooner rather than later. In the case of the 2023 Yamuna floods, the thinking has gone even more moronic. As the existing Hathnikund barrage was unable to handle the river's fury, they're now thinking of building a dam upstream of this. And we all know what happens when dams get aneurysms…

Cities on and near the coast the world over — Mumbai, Kolkata, New York and even London — are today facing the prospect of having to use canoes and motorboats instead of cars as the primary means of transport as sea waters rise due to global warming. True, the annual rise levels may seem low, but the pancake-flat islands in the Pacific like Fiji, the Maldives in the

Indian Ocean and low-lying countries like Bangladesh are right in the firing line. Some have already begun going under. Already sea-level increases have inundated many low-lying islands in the Sunderbans and displaced thousands of people living on them. The coasts of Kerala are being eroded by an increasingly invasive sea, angry perhaps with the sort of 'reclamation' we've been indulging in. And when a sea or ocean is angry, nothing can stop it from doing what it wants. We must remember what the ocean did to the nuclear reactor at Fukushima in Japan after the tsunami — even though this was not caused by global warming. It was as if Mother Nature was just flexing her muscles in warning.

It's not only our part of the world that has experienced devastating floods. Not long back, a power plant and dam in Norway were destroyed and homes and roads were washed away, with ferocious rain and hailstorms sweeping across other Scandinavian and European countries at the height of summer, when people normally take off all their clothes and sunbathe! West Africa, Italy, Pakistan, parts of the United States and China have recently all suffered gargantuan volumes of rain occurring over a very short time, flooding major cities like Beijing and New York. Sunny Southern California and even the Death Valley (one of the hottest, driest areas of the world) have experienced — for the first time in their existence — flash floods. This, scientists warn, is soon going to become par for the course.

Fee-Fo-Fire-Fum

And then there's the other side of this diabolical coin: fire! As deadly as floods are wildfires often set off by extreme heat (heatwaves) and drought. In several European countries such as Italy, Spain and Greece, as well as in Africa, the United States and Australia and over wide swathes of Canada, heatwaves have seared, and droughts have skeletonized huge tracts of land and the living, not to mention charred the homes, holiday resorts and lives of those living there. The once paradisiacal island resort town of Lahaina on the island of Maui in Hawaii burned to the ground in an uncontrollable wildfire driven by hurricane-inspired winds of 120 kmph. Remember, Hawaii is a tropical rainforest, not a desiccated desert. Entire towns in Canada have had to be evacuated as the fires billowed towards them relentlessly. Here in India (lest we get too smug) forest fires regularly crackle and race through our mountain forests every year, and it's too dreadful to think what one of these might to do our tinderbox tenement-style hill stations clinging on to the mountainsides for dear life.

I regularly watch natural history documentaries on television and it's amazing how, invariably, shows on African wildlife and parks begin with the voiceover grimly intoning, 'no rain has fallen for the last eight months…' or 'this is the sixth straight year of drought…' While fire quickly kills every living thing in its path, drought kills slowly of hunger and thirst. Animals like elephants have no choice but to walk vast distances in search of hidden sources of water under dried riverbeds which herd matriarchs remember from decades back. Other animals flock to the shrinking waterholes where their predators wait gleefully: but these too have their issues as they fight each other tooth and claw over precious, ever-shrinking suitable territories. Often, it's these droughts that trigger the fires: a bolt of lightning spears down (or diabolically arsonists go to work), setting spark to the tinder-dry savannah grasses and stunted trees, and no downpour follows to quench the conflagration. Fire has always been an integral part of the natural cycle as the ash and charcoal it generates invigorates the soil and permits fresh plant growth, once it rains again. But remember, this is a cycle, not a permanent state of affairs when no rain falls at all for years at a stretch.

Furies All

We have upset and irritated Mother Nature enough to make her lash out in the harshest possible manner. Flood and fire apart, we now have to deal with her apoplectic fury in the form of hurricanes, gales, tornadoes, typhoons and cyclones, and her power knows no bounds. Tornadoes can completely flatten entire towns in a matter of hellish seconds, as effectively as any nuclear device; cyclones and hurricanes flood and level villages, towns, cities and agricultural land on a massive scale. The warming of the oceans is leading to an increase in the frequency of these extreme events: cyclones rarely occurred over the Arabian Sea, now they're regularly forming over it and sweeping over coastal cities like Mumbai. The Bay of Bengal was and is notorious as a cauldron for cyclones, and now these are getting even more powerful and frequent than before. The winds whip up the seas into a towering rage and monstrous waves sweep inland, not only flooding the land but rendering it useless for agriculture for years to come.

The Fossil Fuel Mafiosi

There is a gang of what I call 'master criminals' who, like any mafia, have joined hands with each other and with us to cause all the issues that are responsible for the state our precious potpourri planet is currently in. It started off, of course, with Europe's Industrial Revolution in around 1760, supercharged by the discovery of fossil fuels: oil, gas and coal under our feet and under the seabed. Henry Ford developed the assembly line, mass production followed, cities blossomed, factories flourished and people abandoned the countryside to flock to them, to work, earn, bring up their families and to buy, buy, buy. A 'consumer society' was the kind of society most of the world wanted to live in. Every time I visit a supermarket, I am overwhelmed by the sheer volume and variety of goods on display — and 'on sale'. Who buys all this stuff? Do we really need 1,500 varieties of breakfast cereal or trainers to choose from? Well, there are 8+ billion of us, so evidently, we do — or the stuff would not be on the shelves. And everything on display has been born and packed in a factory through a process of mass production, on fast-moving, regimented and now computer-controlled, robotic assembly lines. All this requires helluva lot of energy and a great deal of infrastructure built upon, and raw materials pillaged from, our potpourri planet.

Cities and towns developed and expanded for these reasons and people flocked to them to make a living. And cities and towns sucked up the resources from the hinterland and open country, from forests and mountains, leaving indigenous people and wildlife living there bereft and forests flattened. People had to be fed, so forests were felled or burned and turned into fields of wheat, rice, maize and barley, soya, sunflowers and tulips, not to mention plantations of tea, coffee, cocoa, palm oil and a hundred other things. Vast grassy plains had to be created on which cattle — for meat — could be fed and fattened — and here the Amazon rainforests paid the highest price, so we could enjoy our hamburgers. Palm oil was discovered to be an elixir that could be used in the commercial production of everything from shampoo to chips, so invaluable rainforests in Indonesia and other Southeast Asian countries were flattened and replaced by regimented rows of palm oil plantations, which will probably cost the gentle-eyed orangutan its very existence on our planet. Indonesia has of late reined in its palm oil exploits, but we in India are already looking avariciously at our rainforests in the northeast for this purpose.

Our primary source of power for all this industrial activity and, most importantly for transport, was and still remains the terrible three – coal, gas and oil – and we could not extract and burn enough of it, to generate electricity that powers all our factories and cools, warms and lights up our homes. Also, we needed raw materials to produce all these lovely things, from five-rupee Bics to Bentleys and Boeings. Those raw materials often lay deep underground or were on the surface and had to be hacked out, mined, excavated, extracted and made usable. Iron ore had to be turned into cast iron or converted into steel, for example. We needed sand, stone, granite and marble for our magnificent edifices and wood for our houses, furniture and stoves and ovens. Worse, we rarely cleaned up the mess we made after extracting these natural resources, leaving devastated wastelands in our wake. Again, all energy-consuming and environment destroying activities.

These natural resources seemed inexhaustible, and we burned them up and fought bloody battles over them, ignoring (initially perhaps out of ignorance, but increasingly deliberately) a reality staring us in the face: burning fossil fuels emitted large amounts of carbon dioxide, water vapor, methane, carbon monoxide and other noxious gases, which not only proved a direct threat to our lungs, but sat over our potpourri planet like a tea cosy, gently and gradually heating it up and over time, causing our planet's natural weather cycles the equivalent of a humungous and chronic tummy upset. Hence, the floods, fire and fury! Since pre-industrial times (1750) global temperatures had already increased by 1.1 degree Celsius and while we hope to restrict the rise to within 1.5 degrees, it seems like we may be heading for a 2-degree rise if not more by the turn of the century. In India, the temperature has already risen by 1.7 degrees Celsius between 1901 and 2018.

The internal combustion engines that power all our cars and other vehicles and industrial machinery and the jet engines that fly our planes are perhaps the leading villains in this landscape, as are giant thermal power plants that burn coal to produce electricity. Yes, modern cars now emit far smaller amounts of greenhouse gases than before, and laws the world over are getting tougher. I once came across an advertisement for a high-performance car – a Porsche, I think it was (which admittedly I admire) – which stated that the exhaust gases emitted by the new model were cleaner than the gases in the ambient air. I didn't know whether this was a tribute to Porsche's amazing squeaky-clean technology or a devastating statement on the terrible quality of the air we now breathe and take for granted!

But when there's money to be made, there are always ways to wink at or dodge the rules – as one giant German auto company, Volkswagen – ironically also the makers of Porsche – was caught doing recently. Others have also since been caught. Also, the sheer number of vehicles being rolled out year after year negates much of the gains we make in advanced engine technology. Besides, more vehicles mean more and broader roads and expressways, which usually come at the cost of forests, mountain slopes and agricultural land, completely upsetting the lives of the animals and people who have lived there for many lifetimes.

It really is an oxymoronic situation: on the one hand we are piously lectured to by our leaders that we must do all we can to protect our planet, to reduce our carbon footprint and emissions: it is our beholden, patriotic duty. On the other hand ministers in charge of industry, as well as big industrialists, are all gung-ho when vehicle manufacturing numbers rise exponentially year on year! We're entering the arena of electric and hydrogen-powered vehicles, but it is still early days (the use of lithium-ion batteries has its own major issues with the environment) to figure out how these will actually pan out. The giant energy companies that extract oil, gas and coal are naturally not too keen to see their often-profligate profits take a dip; they use their muscle, money and political connections to ensure that any promising self-sustaining source of energy is stifled at birth. And anyway, it's been claimed that tires produce more particulate pollution than the exhausts of modern fuel-efficient cars, and this is especially so with the heavier battery-powered electric vehicles whose tires wear out quicker.

Halo, Halo Shining Bright/ On the Hypocrites of the Night

Of course, there are ginormous double standards at play here: the developed West, after having colonized and ravaged entire continents and consumed and fattened themselves on gargantuan amounts of their rich natural resources (wood, minerals, precious metals, building material, oil, spices, tea and coffee), are now wagging fingers at us and telling us to reduce our carbon emissions: our livestock belch too much methane, they say (which they do), and the coal we burn is dirty. Like any outraged teenager, we're now retorting angrily: hey, just hold on there, bro, now it's our turn to develop using whichever energy source is available, economical and most convenient (still mostly coal), so you go and suck eggs, and in fact pay for what you took from us and for your profligate habits and the damage they have caused. They really ought to, because the moral ground they stand on is nothing but quicksand: we often praise the British for the railway network they set up all across India, which involved the mass felling of forests for laying down railway sleepers. Well, they didn't do it so you could go visit your nani; they built it so they could move looted raw materials and resources to the nearest port, from where they could be shipped away to Britain.

Many of those fat-cat, tight-fisted countries are of course loath to pay up, but hopefully will have a change of heart once they themselves feel the effects of climate change directly — as many have already started doing — and that scientists promise will continue more severely. Happily, many youngsters the world over, including those from the developed nations, are now beginning to raise their voices and shake their fists as they realize what seems to lie in store, as well as use their brains to find ways to avoid a patently unpleasant and very insecure future.

Certainly, it is our turn to 'develop' but we can't do it by biting off our noses to spite our faces — which is what we seem to be doing now. I have never understood why 'development' is always pitted as a rival against 'environment', and that in order to develop we have no choice but to destroy our environment. If we don't have a healthy environment to live in, clean air to breathe and pure water to drink, there is no development at all, only destruction. And we can't do to ourselves what the West did to us: ravage and pillage our own country.

Smog Ho Jai!

Oh yes, the West had their issues too, like the famous London pea-soup fogs that started off in the thirteenth century due to coal burning factories and continued as the Industrial Revolution took off in around 1760, right up to the famous smog of 1953. Another pea-souper event occurred in 1962, after which a legislation was passed, the implementation of which since has resulted in much cleaner air. We have to live with the mess we are now creating for ourselves by so casually bypassing the laws to make it easier for us to rip up, raid and destroy our natural landscapes.

In 2019, India emitted around 6.6–7 per cent of the worldwide global emissions of greenhouse gases (China leads with 27 per cent, followed by the United States with 11 per cent). And thanks to our humungous population, our per capita contribution is around 2 tonnes of carbon dioxide, half of the world's average. But there's no point in hiding behind this statistic, because like it or not, in 2015 we were the fourth most susceptible country that suffered from the ill-effects of climate change: it's caused the Himalayan glaciers to retreat and melt and scientists are warning that the mighty Indus, Ganges and Brahmaputra might eventually run dry in the decades to come. That would be truly catastrophic.

The main source of all that carbon dioxide and other noxious gases we put out is coal, though gas, oil, wood burning and biomass burning contribute solidly as well. If we clean up our act, it's said, the benefits we will accrue (in terms of better health, for example) will be four to five times as much as the costs we may thereby incur. In other words, it's more than worth it!

We're not the only ones recklessly loosening our drawstrings, so to speak! Recently the United Kingdom has opened up more than 100 new sites in the North Sea to drilling for oil and gas and has pushed back its target to stop the manufacture of cars powered by internal combustion engines from 2030 to 2035, a move which, apart from causing a furore among environmentalists, also has the auto industry fuming because they had been planning and investing for a 2030 transition!

Today being outdoors can be dangerous to your health. Ninety per cent of the world's population breathes dirty air and pollution emanating directly from fossil fuel usage, which kills an estimated 3.61 million people every year. (Overall, the toll from air pollution is 7 million.) Other sources of airborne pollution: industry, mainly cement and iron and steel plants; and agriculture, in part due to the increase in the use of fertilizer, crop burning and waste. The bill? Five trillion dollars per year, not exactly pin money!

Delhi is always near the top five cities in the world when it comes to air pollution, often in a gasp-and-gasp race with Beijing and Shanghai for the top spot. The blame has been laid at several doors – stubble burning in the fields of adjoining states, the sheer exponential increase in the number of vehicles on the roads (apparently more than 1,000 new cars hit the roads of

Delhi, every day!), unfortunate wind direction or the lack of breeze altogether to blow away the fumes. Whatever the reason may be, choking smog still engulfs the city especially in winter, and doctors inform us that we're smoking so many packets of cigarettes a day, without ever lighting up a single stick. Leave the city, they advise us, or stay indoors, with your air filters switched on! (I do, I flee to Goa!) But what a way to live (even though it is still balmy in Goa)!

Our Sacred Sewers

Probably there is not a single river in India that today is not polluted. Most are just big, sludgy, odiferous sewers with near-zero levels of oxygen. Several large cities are built along the banks of major rivers, and most of these cities are responsible for the major pollution load that those rivers carry and eventually take to the ocean. In Delhi, when the Yamuna enters the city from the north, you can still see the riverbed in the shallows. By the time it passes through the city, 22 kilometres downstream it is usually covered by a thick blanket of stinking, toxic foam and there is absolutely no dissolved oxygen in the water for any living creature to breathe. Fortunes have been spent (or been quietly pocketed) to clean up the Yamuna over the years, to little effect: industrial units continue to spew toxic pollutants into the drains that run into the river, untreated sewage flows unhampered, rich with faecal bacteria. In 2023, some 715 million gallons of sewage was dumped into the Yamuna every single day, of which 245 million gallons remained untreated.

Certainly, cleansing operations are conducted. Every year, scores of schoolchildren, NGOs and concerned citizens are rounded up to 'clean up' the Yamuna, usually spearheaded by moralizing, sanctimonious political bigwigs. Piles of garbage and filth are triumphantly dredged out and everyone leaves feeling that they've done something good for the environment. Next year, they're back on the job!

There is a simple solution to this, which Bittu Sahgal, the renowned editor of Sanctuary Magazine once brilliantly illustrated with an example: a moron was taking a bath and getting annoyed because his bathtub kept overflowing. He tried baling out the surplus, but the tub kept filling up. So, he yelled to his wife for help. She walked in, took one look and leaned over and shut the taps. Problem solved.

We unfortunately are not shutting off the taps. That is a question that all those poor schoolchildren and students, knee-deep in stinking sludge, should demand an answer to from all the smug, smiling political bigwigs that conduct these 'cleansing operations' every year: 'Uncleji, but why is the river getting dirty like this every time?' And then, 'First shut off the taps, then we'll clean it!' Nothing like being publicly put in your place by a cheeky schoolkid who has a bullseye point to make!

There's another factor here that I've never been able to work my head around. So many great rivers in India are regarded as sacred — led by the Ganges, whose waters we believe will wash away our sins. Even these holy rivers, in reality, are nothing but sewers. Adding to the multitude of sins we dump in them every day are the bodies of dead animals, semi-cremated human beings, toxic wastes and heavy metals from industrial units and tanneries, solid waste, sewage — the works. Surely any holy water body ought to be crystal clear; it's bad enough that they must wash away our sins! Again, fortunes have been allegedly spent on cleaning up the rivers, but the results are plain to see.

Cities abroad *have* cleaned up their rivers. The Thames flowing through London, which was notoriously filthy, has been cleaned up, as has been the Seine flowing under the bridges of Paris! (That too in time for the 2024 Olympics: it was an enormous, expensive, time-consuming undertaking, but it has been done, though residents claimed that the river was still not clean or safe enough to swim in.) In the United States, General Electric and other industrial units dumped carcinogenic toxic waste into the Hudson for years, before the United States Environment Protection Agency, in accordance with the 1972 Clean Air Act, stepped in. Apart from General Electric that was made to clean up its mess, every industrial unit along the course of the river was checked for the effluents they emitted and made to clean up their act. In August 2023 British endurance swimmer Lewis Pugh swam the entire length of the Hudson to show that it was now clean and safe enough to dip your toes into! Recently the illegal panning for gold along sections of the Amazon is causing mercury pollution in that mighty river, which is fatal for all life. We in India too have a long, long way to go.

Incinerate!

The dumping (and burning, deliberately or otherwise) of solid waste is another contributor to unhealthy air and an unhealthy environment. Delhi has at least two notorious 'multi-storeyed' garbage dumps, which simmer and stink throughout the year. The only glimmer of hope around these dumps is the enormous unorganized (but not disorganized) recycling industry they spawn. Waste is collected, sorted and recycled, and we in India are past-masters at jugaad, so a lot of thrown-away stuff gets a second chance to be useful again.

Plastic Has Turned Drastic

In 1907, a scientist called Leo Hendrik Baekeland made the world's first fully synthetic plastic, which he called Bakelite, and nothing was the same again. One variety of plastic based on cellulose (which, ironically, is naturally biodegradable) had earlier been created by one Alexander Parkes and exhibited at the Great International Exhibition in London in 1862, but it was Baekeland who was called the 'father of the plastics industry'. It was, as most plastics today are, a fossil-fuel based synthetic material, which in its various avatars, could be moulded, extracted and shaped any way you liked, each being made using modern industrial methods relying on fossil fuels as its main raw material. Plastic was light, strong and cheap. It could be made as pliable as a dragonfly's wing, strong enough to resist a toddler's attempt at destruction, and had a hundred million uses it could be put to: from ubiquitous carry bags and bottles, to car bumpers, airplane windows (stretched acrylic), furniture, Lego bricks and of course, Barbie dolls. In 1997, the pop group Aqua brought out their hit number 'Barbie Girl', which belted out, 'I'm a Barbie girl/ In a Barbie world/ Life in plastic / Is fantastic!' Alas, too fantastic for its, and our, own good, because there was just one hitch: after using it we just couldn't get rid of it. We crushed it, smashed it, melted it down, burned it (emitting hugely toxic fumes) and buried it, but it just refused to decompose and disappear on its own. So, we've been dumping a hell of a lot of it in our rivers and oceans — over 8 million metric tonnes of it every year — and burying more of it in landfills. We're currently producing over 350 million tonnes of plastic waste every year, a figure which is expected to reach (if we go on as is) to 1 billion tonnes by 2060. Further projections are truly frightening: if we continue gung-ho, by 2050 plastic could belch out 56 billion tonnes of greenhouse gas emissions; by 2100 this could be 260 billion tonnes.

Plastic's major contribution to global warming stems from the fact that it is fossil-fuel based. A 2019 report stated that the production and incineration of plastic and plastic waste contributed greenhouse gases to the tune of 850 million tonnes of carbon dioxide into the atmosphere, a figure that could rise to 1.34 billion tonnes of carbon dioxide by 2030. And it is awful for the planet's and our health and well-being in several other ways. Large bits of plastic (say in the form of jerrycans and shampoo bottles) float around in the ocean, for years and years, caught in swirling circular currents. Many bits of flotsam and jetsam are swallowed by fishes, dolphins and whales (playing havoc with their tummies!), others get broken into smaller pieces due to abrasion and even smaller particles may sink to the seabed and enter the food chain via the tiny creatures that may consume them. Plastics kill an estimated 1 million seabirds every year, and 100,000 marine mammals, which get entangled in nylon fishing nets and drown. Ninety per cent of all seabirds have plastic debris in their gut. By some estimates, there could be more plastic in the ocean than fish, by weight, by 2050.

Apart from entanglement, there are lethal toxicological effects as well as suffocation and starvation that is caused by plastic pollution. Organisms may hitch on to plastics and be borne into areas outside of their normal habitats

and ecosystems, and cause havoc in these new areas and ecosystems, upsetting the stable ecological equations that prevail there. This can impact fisheries, human health and tourism.

The United States produces the most plastic pollution – some 42 million tonnes of waste every year. Many developed countries in the past had been conveniently dumping their plastic waste on to developing countries to sort out and deal with – until in 2013, an amendment to what was called the Basel Convention (on the transportation of hazardous wastes) was made to prevent this from happening, and to which nearly all countries signed up. In 2022, 175 countries promised to attempt to frame laws by 2024, aimed at ending plastic pollution. So let us see what comes of it!

Perhaps the most visible manifestation of plastic pollution in the ocean is that of the great plastic 'garbage patches' that are found floating in the oceans. One of the largest is the Great Pacific Garbage Patch that lies well off the coast of Hawaii. Formed by the action of the oceans' currents these floating horrors are a testimony to our wasteful ways. Attempts are being made to corral these garbage patches with the help of gigantic funnel- and net-like devices, to collect and sort out the garbage so it can be properly dealt with and perhaps recycled. As rivers are a major source of plastic pollution (because we dump our bottles and plastic bags in them and they carry them to the ocean) the sources of some such rivers (our Ganges is one victim) are being monitored so that the plastic can be intercepted before it rides out onto the high seas.

But plastic — and plastic pollution — is everywhere. Take a train journey anywhere in India and you will see that the sides of the tracks are festooned with innumerable dirty plastic bags — fluttering from bushes, trees, electric pylons and every visible structure. Oddly they make me think of the flags of political parties, put up during election time!

There are eco-friendly plastic alternatives, even if they have a long way to go before becoming mainstream: biodegradable plastics degrade in the sun, on exposure to ultraviolet radiation, or water and dampness. Enzymes, bacteria and attacks by insects such as mealworms and waxworms could also make them degrade. Starch powder has also been tried as an additive to assist degradation of normal plastic, but apparently it doesn't do the job fully! Bioplastics, which use naturally degradable plant material like cellulose and starch are another option, but still have a very long way to go. We now make an estimated 327,000 tonnes of bioplastic annually the world over, as against 150 million tonnes of fossil-fuel based plastics.

Personally, I've always thought we should take our cues from nature. Three of the toughest, lightest substances in nature: chitin, cellulose and keratin are all biodegradable – even if they may take their time about it. Chitin is what the exoskeleton of insects is made from: light, strong and waterproof. Cellulose is what plant structures, like wood, are made of: indigestible to most (except termites), and again immensely strong. Our hair, nails, the claws and beaks of birds and animals, their fur, spiders' silk are all made from keratin. Willy-nilly we will have to be soon looking at these options, as fossil fuels are not going to last forever, even if the plastics we fashion from them look as though they will.

The planet today has probably never been as aware of climate change and global warming than ever before in its history. Every news bulletin these days, every newspaper and of course the social media have tales to tell, connected to the subject – usually involving the infamous five discussed above. And within society the world over it has caused deep rifts. There are those who flatly deny the fact of global warming and climate change. All this is nonsense, they claim, look at the past – the earth has warmed and cooled multiple times over the millennia. (But has it done so as fast and furiously as now?) Also, they argue, at present there is no real alternative to the use of fossil fuels for our energy requirements: the alternative sources of energy are still far too meagre to produce the energy we require, and more expensive. At the other end of the spectrum are those that are shrieking that the end of the world is nigh, that we ought to stop drilling for oil and gas as of now (which, is not going to happen). Like it or not, we are going to have to transition to alternate, renewable sources of energy because fossil fuels are not going to last forever. Let's just hope we do not destroy most of life on our potpourri planet in the meanwhile: already we're being warned that the Sixth Great Extinction event is under way, and that we are chiefly responsible for it. And also that its ramifications can be irreversible and deadly for all life on the planet — including ours.

CHAPTER 2: FOREVER GONE

Scientists tell us that we're in the midst of the Sixth Mass Extinction event, which will prove disastrous to life on earth. A 'mass extinction event' is one in which most of life on earth dies out in relatively quick time: bacteria, fungi, plants, reptiles, animals, amphibians, fish, invertebrates and heck, maybe even humans. So, we may think that pfft, one day, every living thing on our potpourri planet will just roll over and die. Not nice at all, but not so fast either! 'Quick time' in geological terms could span thousands and even millions of years, so there's no need to pack one's bags right now and look around helplessly wondering if there is a flight to Mars or the Moon! Also, as this is the sixth time that it is happening, it means that the previous five mass extinction events did not manage to totally end life on earth: life came back, evolved differently perhaps, but it came back and thrived once more. The last mass extinction event occurred some 65.5 million years ago, when a rogue meteorite crashed into the Yucatan Peninsula in Mexico (causing the Chicxulub crater) and wiped out the dinosaurs and a lot of other living things. But the littler creatures survived the holocaust, and continued to evolve as time went by.

A meteorite with a wayward sense of direction caused the last extinction event. This one is being hugely aided and abetted by our activities. We're turbocharging it so it's happening at warp speed and that is what is worrying scientists and biologists (and should be worrying us too). In fact, in the last 100 to 200 years the loss of biodiversity has been so rapid that some conservation biologists believe that it is our activities that have set off the extinction event.

Certainly, our activities have changed the face of the earth: we've used land, water and energy unsustainably, causing the climate change we're now experiencing. As much as 40 per cent of all land has been converted to agricultural use, which is also responsible for 90 per cent of the deforestation that's happened, and sucks up 70 per cent of the earth's freshwater resources. (Of course, we need to feed ourselves, but you get the scale of the issue.) Poor food production and consumption patterns and habits have significantly contributed to greenhouse gas emissions, which are now heating up our planet and causing mayhem around the world, with wayward weather patterns upsetting food production and harvest schedules. It really is a kind of vicious circle: we indulge in unsustainable agricultural practices that pump up the level of greenhouse gases, which cause temperatures to rise further, causing droughts or floods which, in turn, are obviously not good for food production, thus causing hunger and thirst all round as well as wars and refugee crises. And to counter these, we indulge in yet more unsustainable agricultural practices.

These irresponsible practices have naturally affected not only human beings but all living creatures on the planet. They have destroyed the homes and habitats of thousands of species, making many of these face a one-way future. Some believe that one million species worldwide are now in one way or another looking down the barrel of the gun.

Breaking the Chain

So why should we care if one or another worm, beetle or wasp or even the polar bear goes extinct? How will it affect our lives, especially if we have nothing to do with the creatures? Well, as the late Gerald Durrell kept pointing out, think of nature as one massive web, with each strand in the web representing a living creature. If one of the strands were to snap, it would cause the web to tremble a little, and maybe make the adjacent strand tremble and eventually snap. And then a chain reaction would start, which would eventually destroy the whole web. I like to think that this is really the world wide web of life.

All life on planet earth is interconnected: the classic example of course is the one that is provided by apex predators, like tigers. If tigers went extinct, the herbivores would make merry and have far too many babies who would eat up all the foliage, causing their populations to eventually crash, because all too soon there'd be nothing left for them to eat, and similarly disastrously affect the lives of all the other animals, insects, fungi et al. that depend on green leaves and shoots to live. The forests themselves would die, shorn of energy-producing green leaves. And then where would we be?

Sometimes of course, evolution sort of paints itself into a corner: the great banyan tree, or kalpavriksh (the tree of life), our national tree, like all the rest of trees in the around 1,000-strong fig family, depends on its own bespoke species of fig wasp to pollinate it. The fig wasp in turn depends on the banyan to have its babies in. If we, in our reckless, lackadaisical way, were to kill off the fig wasp (say by means of a pesticide), there'd be nothing to pollinate the banyan. Eventually all the banyans would die out – without leaving any heirs. And this could mean the end of the road for many of the denizens of the forests.

You see, the banyan and other fig species are sort of the grandees of the forest, the big dada dons. They fruit at different times of the year, and animals and birds flock to them for their largesse. This means that there is never a lean period, as there would be if the trees fruited seasonally as so many others do. So, there is always food available somewhere in the forest at all times. Birds of all species throw parties, scoffing up the drupes and the insects hovering around them; high up on the branches, monkeys stuff their faces and cheek pouches, and down below deer, wild boar and antelope vacuum up the spilled drupes that fall like manna from heaven. They thrive, which means that tigers, leopards and lions can enjoy plenty of fresh venison, jackals, hyenas and vultures can enjoy their leftovers and ants and other insects can clean up the bones, all this leading to a healthily functioning ecosystem.

The birds and animals also help in afforestation by undertaking their own 'tree planting drives'. They scoff up the figs, and we all know what figs can do (prunes are dried figs, by the way!): so sooner rather than later, they all have to go do potty. Which they do, far and wide in the jungle. The undigested seeds are scattered over the forest floor, some landing on the branches of other unfortunate trees, and they begin their lives as baby banyans...

The case of the banyan and fig wasp also illustrates just how careful we have to be while dealing with nature. A careless decision, like the introduction of a new pesticide without proper research, could wipe out those bespoke fig wasps, and now we know the consequences. Of course, it would have been nice had the banyan not depended on just a single bespoke species of wasp, but genes (here the wasps' especially) as we know only evolve in ways that benefit themselves exclusively.

Killing Them Quickly

Really, it is so easy to screw up, even unwittingly. Look what happened with the vultures. An analgesic, diclofenac, given to livestock (we use it ourselves too for muscle pain relief) to help them produce more milk, remained in the carcasses after the animals had died. Vultures dining off the carcasses – usually left to rot outside villages – ingested it, and it destroyed their kidneys. One would imagine that vultures, which have amongst the most potent of stomach acids, would have been able to deal with a simple analgesic, but there you are. The result: a 95–99 per cent collapse in the population of vultures in our region. And with no vultures around, the carcasses continued to rot and breed dangerous bacteria and pathogens, or were consumed by feral dogs, whose population exploded. And they, of course hunted down other animals and birds too, leading to population declines. Worse, they carried rabies, which they spread to us. Nor were they as good as the vultures had been in cleaning up the carcasses, leaving bits to fester, so eventually the pathogens got into drinking water supplies. According to one report by *CBS News*, urban areas with large livestock populations, more people died in those areas where the livestock had been treated with diclofenac, rather than in others. It estimates that between 2000 and 2005, the death of vultures en masse caused as many as 500,000 additional human deaths.

We should never underestimate how dangerous we can be. Two of the world's once most populous species, the passenger pigeon and the grand American buffalo, serve as examples of this. The passenger pigeons, endemic to America, could darken skies with their numbers as they flew over, more than 2 billion in a single flock. When they perched on branches, they broke them, because they were so many of them. It's thought that no bird species existed in such large numbers ever before, or for that matter ever will again. Sadly, passenger pigeons were good eating. So, the Americans brought out their guns and shot them and shot them and shot them, and raided their nests for eggs, probably convinced that here was an endless supply of tasty, very cheap meat and scrambled eggs. In 1879 a billion birds were caught (and presumably eaten) in the state of Michigan. The end result of this carnage? Martha, the last passenger pigeon on our potpourri planet, died in the Cincinnati Zoo on 1 September, 1914.

The great shaggy American buffaloes that thundered over the vast plains of America in their thousands and provided sustenance to the Native Americans were all but shot to extinction by the white man, whose intentions here were certainly mala fide. Of course, they shot the bison for its meat and shaggy coat, but they also shot it for the heck of it, often just leaning out of their passing railroad carriage windows and blazing away. So much so that passengers had to cover their noses while passing through these areas because of the stench of rotting meat. One of the buffalo-killing 'heroes' was Buffalo Bill Cody, whose exploits exceeded those of some of the British viceroys and Indian royalty regarding tigers, lions, cheetahs and waterfowl in India. But worst of all, the white colonizers of America wanted deliberately to exterminate the buffalo in order to starve the Native Americans who depended on them and whose lands they had devoured and plundered. Thankfully some good sense prevailed and the great shaggy beasts were accorded protection and small fractions of the great herds of yore still rumble across the grassy plains.

We in India ought not to be batting our eyes sanctimoniously considering what we and our erstwhile colonial rulers and maharajas have done to our national animal, the Royal Bengal Tiger. From 100,000 tigers in 1900, the numbers dropped to around 40,000 in the 1950s, plummeting to just over 1,400 in 2006, and to just under 4,000 animals now. Project Tiger launched in 1972 by then Prime Minister Indira Gandhi, and the Wildlife (Protection) Act introduced in the same year, did a lot to bring the tiger (and other animals) back from the brink of extinction, but the threat remains: the moment we let our guard down, matters go into a tailspin. It happened in Sariska and Panna, both tiger reserves and national parks supposed to be accorded the highest level of security to the tiger. After stubborn po-faced official denials (aided by imaginary census numbers), and the banishment of whistleblowers, it had to be finally admitted that these tiger reserves had zero tigers by 2009, all the animals having fallen to poachers' bullets. As of May 2024, Sariska had forty tigers; in 2022, Panna had between fifty-seven and sixty tigers, signalling successful rehabilitation and protection since the debacle. A similar fate was encountered by the grand one-horned Indian rhinoceros, hunted down to double figures, and whose numbers in Kaziranga National Park in Assam (their stronghold) dropped to twelve in 1908. The Asiatic lion too escaped by the skin of its teeth, its numbers too down to an abysmal dozen or so animals at the turn of the century, hiding out in its last stronghold in the Junagadh district of Gujarat, before it was accorded protection. So far, you may say, we have been lucky, as we haven't lost any wild megafauna (except the cheetah, which we are now trying desperately to reintroduce from Africa), but we still seemingly haven't learned anything from the past. Today the superbly supercilious Great Indian Bustard (which Salim Ali proposed be our national bird, for sound ecological reasons) seems to be heading for the end of the road as barely over 100 wild birds remain, and they must evade the giant propellers of windmills and sizzling power lines which have encroached upon their territories. They do not have very good forward vision, so can't see these impediments ahead of them as they fly.

Meanwhile, we continue to fragment forest habitats, bulldozing into them on various pretexts, corralling the animals in smaller and smaller patches of forest, with no corridors they can use to get from one forest to another. This prevents the healthy migration and mixing of genes between populations, leading to genetic inbreeding. Also, we're ramming expressways through these protected areas, putting up monoculture plantations in place of healthy mixed forests, and as described in the previous chapter, have now considerably watered down the laws, making it easier for so-called development activities and tourism to invade, disrupt, disfigure and destroy these areas.

Bringing Them Back

Captive breeding is one way by which extremely endangered species can be brought back from the brink. Precious specimens are caught, kept in enclosures and hopefully breed — in zoos and safari parks. When the population increases and stabilizes, they are released back into their original habitats, where hopefully they will continue to have families! But one of the main factors that makes a captive-breeding and rehabilitation programme a success is that there still must be a wild original habitat where the animals bred in captivity can be released. If the original habitat has been turned into an industrial estate, tourist destination or theme park, or destroyed by mining — well, the animal is not going to be very happy, to say the least. Captive breeding and habitat maintenance and rehabilitation go hand in hand.

This, in fact, forms part of the concept of 'rewilding', which has become very popular in the West. Rewilding is basically the restoration of huge swathes of natural habitats to their original states, the establishing of corridors between them and, if necessary, the re-introduction of apex predators or keystone species to them. To give back to nature the habitats we took from her (and usually despoiled) along with the animals (like wolves in

Yellowstone National Park), which were responsible for their well-being. The problem with 'rewilding' in India is that we do not have vast swathes of wilderness areas – people and wildlife in our country often live cheek by jowl and forests are fragmented, with little scope of creating corridors between them. But we have had some limited successes: the re-introduction of tigers to Sariska and Panna for example, and that of the nearly-extinct Pygmy hog in Assam – after having restored their grassland habitats. Other successes were the re-introduction of rhinos to the Manas National Park from where they had been exterminated due to insurgency and the captive breeding of vultures, which went hand in hand with the banning of diclofenac for veterinary use – the analgesic that slaughtered them. But successful 'rewilding' can only happen if the ecosystems are restored and maintained to their original pristine condition, and there is political will and intelligence, backed by financial support.

Rewilding can also be done in urban landscapes: the creation of the Yamuna Biodiversity Park and Aravalli Biodiversity Park in Delhi being two such examples, where devastated landscapes have been restored. Unfortunately, in neighbouring Haryana, plans are being hatched to convert vast areas of the Aravallis into a massive safari-park-cum-zoo (cum-open-air circus?), starring hippos and probably giraffes from Africa, which would be the very opposite of rewilding.

One major issue with releasing captive-bred animals into the wild, especially in a crowded country like India, is that if they are familiar with us and unafraid, there may be more human-wildlife conflict. There is quite enough of this happening with 'normal' wild animals, as we continue to barge into and take over their territories. But captive-bred animals, already used to us, may not be wary enough and may invade our spaces (which, invariably, we would have grabbed from them originally), scaring the bejesus out of us, and may think nothing of dining off our livestock or foodgrains. The end result: relocation to another area (where they might run into trouble with the resident animals), incarceration in a zoo or death. But certainly, in some cases (like the Arabian oryx, mentioned below) captive-breeding programmes have saved the animals from extinction.

We must also be aware that captive breeding may not work every time. The population of wild, irascible Tasmanian devils in New Zealand plummeted by 90 per cent due to a transmissible form of cancer called devil facial tumour disease. A captive-breeding devil programme was launched in Australia, but it was found that the breeding success of captive-bred females was less than what was required, meaning that you could not depend on this programme alone to guarantee a future for the animals.

Of course, animals, plants, insects et al. of all kinds go extinct naturally. But it's being said that currently the extinction rate of species is between 1,000 and 10,000 times the natural rate — so we're the ones that have recklessly put the pedal to the metal. It is time we eased off if we want to stave off potentially catastrophic situations. If for example, we cause the complete collapse of bee populations around the world (already colony collapses are regularly happening), it could have devastating impacts on food production and economies, triggering off all sorts of very unpleasant situations indeed all around the world.

Today, according to the IUCN, as many as 16,306 species of animals in the world are endangered.

Also, we have no right to cause any species on the planet to go extinct: it is morally reprehensible. And certainly at least not until we are able to bring it back to life. (Fear not, work is even being done towards this goal: we want the woolly mammoth back, and are attempting to develop a mammoth-elephant hybrid. The recreation of pedigreed mammoths however still seems to be far away!)

Happily, we are all not just sitting back on our haunches watching animals, birds, insects and plants just sign out one by one. All over the world, there are scores of projects aimed at saving species that at teetering on the brink. Indeed, this noble intention has been the raison d'etre behind the existence of many zoos around the world – in San Diego, Jersey (the Channel Islands), Singapore and several other places. Captive breeding is their mantra, though as mentioned earlier, often this is easier said than done. But several species have been saved from a sticky end and even been re-introduced to their original homes once their numbers stabilized.

One of the earliest re-introduction programmes was that of the handsome Arabian oryx launched way back in 1962 by the Phoenix Zoo in Arizona, United States, with financial aid from the WWF. The entire surviving wild population of nine animals was sent to the zoo at that time. By the 1970s these animals had been hunted to extinction in the wild. At the zoo over a period of time, 240 oryx were born and sent to other zoos. By 1980 it was thought that these animals could go back home – to their deserts in the Middle East. While they did well enough in fenced-in reserves in Saudi Arabia, they met a dreadful fate in Oman, which reflected exactly the mindset of so many governments around the world today: the government of Oman opened up 90 per cent of the of Oman's Arabian Oryx Sanctuary to oil prospecting, and the oryx population in that place promptly went into freefall. From 450 animals in 1996, the population crashed to sixty-five animals in 2007, and now no fewer than four breeding pairs remain. Worldwide, the wild population as of 2016 was estimated at 1,220 animals (of which 850 are mature individuals), with another 6000–7000 in zoos around the world.

Other successful reintroduction programs include that of the magnificent Californian condor, Przewalski's horse in Mongolia, the golden lion tamarin in Central America and the cheetah in South Africa. The Galapagos tortoise was once down to twelve individuals, but thanks to captive breeding the number is now over 2,000.

Plants too are being preserved. The Millenium Seed Bank in the Kew Gardens in the United Kingdom has 2.4 billion seeds belonging to over 39,000 plant species, stored in deep freezes in bomb- and radiation-proof underground vaults. The seeds have come from over ninety-seven countries and serve as an insurance policy against disaster.

If we can do that with seeds, we can and are doing it with animals. It's called cryopreservation. The Zoological Society of San Diego has set up a 'frozen zoo' where the sperm, eggs and embryos of the world's most endangered animals are deep-frozen and stored in vaults, in the hope that if the need arises the creatures can be 're-created' from these. So far more than 355 species of mammals, reptiles, birds, et al. have been preserved. All this sounds very dire and doomsday-ish but it's just a kind of insurance policy, in case the worst happens.

We must never forget what Big Mama Nature gives us if allowed to do her work uninterrupted: clean water, fresh air, rich soil, protection against extreme weather and flooding. As also raising our spirits like nothing else (including retail therapy) can do. Back in 1997, ecological-economist Robert Constanza, professor at UCL Institute for Global Prosperity, University College London, and his team calculated the worth of nature conservation to be $44 trillion at today's prices — not a figure to be sneezed at but one that most politicians and cost-benefit accountants fail to take heed of, when they condemn yet another forest to the axe. Also, we must always remember, that even a trillion-gazillion dollars will be unable to replace a single species that goes extinct. Once gone, is forever gone.

Thankfully, there are thousands of people, institutions and organizations around the world who are not prepared to let that happen to other living creatures, and who are determined to ensure that our beautiful potpourri planet does not turn into a hellish desiccated wasted world thanks to climate change, global warming, deforestation and pollution. They do not want their children and grandchildren to inherit a planet where the joy for life has been toxically choked and smothered to death, and where their brains are filled with lead and the only animals they see are in pictures. Some huge international organizations and institutions work around the world and around the clock, others are regional, thousands are localized to relatively small areas — but all are equally relevant. Finally, and most importantly, of course there is an entire army of outraged and horrified individuals who have taken up cudgels for the cause, and some have remarkable achievements to their credit, to the extent of making entire nations change their laws. We'll meet some of them and check out the work they're doing and have done in the following chapter.

CHAPTER 3: OF WHISTLEBLOWERS AND GATEKEEPERS

Good Gatekeepers and Bad

People in power usually do not like whistleblowers, and most governments around the world are themselves gatekeepers — they ensure that ordinary citizens are not privy to unpalatable truths (often about them). But with our potpourri planet being in the mess that it is, this stance cannot be tenable for long, and many countries around the world have thankfully realized this. You can't fool all the people all the time; you can't say there is no storm or hurricane when a wind of 200 kmph is shrieking 'hello?' around your ears. So back in late 1988, the World Meteorological Organization and the United Nations Environment Programme held hands and gave birth to the Inter-governmental Panel on Climate Change (IPCC), headquartered in Geneva, Switzerland. The IPCC was, you could say, issued its official birth certificate by the United Nations the following year. It now has 195 member states (including India), and its mandate is simple: to tell the people of our potpourri planet what the situation is regarding climate change, where we will be heading if we continue in our usual way, and how to mitigate and slow down some of the more unpleasant, if not disastrous, impacts of this. Every six or seven years (called a cycle), it comes out with a kind of report card on the situation, and it has, in 2021, brought out its sixth such report card, formally called the Sixth Assessment Report. It is on the basis of these reports that climate negotiations are conducted annually by the United Nations Framework Convention on Climate Change (UNFCCC), and their Fifth Assessment Report was greatly influential in achieving the landmark Paris Agreement of 2015.

The IPCC harnesses the brains of the best in the field from around the world for the job, so as to be as objective as possible. Their findings are subject to strict scrutiny from peers in their field. Three 'working groups' have been formed, each with its own mandate, as well as a 'task force', which carries out the scientific work.

Working Group I focuses on the physical science involved in shaping climate change – in the past, present and future. Scientists around the world have done a lot of work in trying to understand how climate change works and how human activity has affected it. So, they have studied greenhouse gases and aerosols in the atmosphere, temperature changes on land, in the ocean and in the air, hydrology (the movement, distribution and management of water on our planet), changing weather patterns such as the monsoon as well as extreme weather events like hurricanes and droughts, the changes in the ice sheets and ocean levels, and so on. In short, it attempts to provide a complete picture of the world's climate system and the changes it is undergoing.

If we know what the big picture looks like, we can take steps (hopefully) to meet the challenges posed by climate change, both at the global level and at the regional level. This working group is also examining and assessing how much carbon we can emit (much less than we currently are) in order to meet our climate change targets. It also looks at our energy needs.

Working Group II looks into how vulnerable people and natural ecosystems are to climate change; how it affects people's lives economically, socially and culturally and what it does to forests, grasslands, wetlands and other natural ecosystems. This group also makes suggestions as to how we can adapt to these changes — basically what we need to do to reduce the negative impacts of climate change and to create a self-sustaining planet.

Working Group III concentrates on the areas where Working Group II leaves off: on ways to reduce and mitigate greenhouse gas emissions and remove them altogether from the atmosphere. So, it is looking into the sources of greenhouse gases: energy, transport, construction, waste management, farming methods, industry and forestry. It studies what governments and the private sector can do in the near future and what the world must aim towards for the distant future. It analyses how we can mitigate climate change, taking into account the costs involved, the ability of countries and governments to pay those costs and how acceptable those mitigating moves are to the societies they are applied to.

So, as one can see they have their work cut out for them. The news forthcoming from the IPCC, published in the form of very systematic and detailed reports, has not been very positive, and as one major British newspaper wrote, is 'the starkest warning yet' of 'major inevitable and irreversible climate changes'. Basically, if we continue the way we are going, we are going to be in very deep and hot trouble in the very near future. There are some startling facts, figures and statistics it has provided to which I have added bluntly the implications that are likely to follow.

Our increasing appetite for land, be it for 'food, fibre, feed, timber and energy' has 'negatively affected' areas that are ice-free. Approximately 25–30 per cent of the total food we produce is criminally wasted or lost, and while 821 million people around the world are malnourished, as many as 2 billion are, well, overfed. But yes, we can reduce the amount of land we need for food production by choosing what we grow wisely, and of course by not throwing so much of it uneaten into the garbage bin. This trend of binning perfectly edible food is especially prevalent in the developed world and can now be seen even in countries like India.

Thanks to our activities, global surface temperatures have shot up in the last fifty years, much more than they did in the any other fifty-year period for the last two thousand years, and this has begun causing havoc in various ways.

In the ten years before 2020, deaths from extreme weather events such as floods, droughts and storms were fifteen times greater in areas that were more vulnerable to them (and less able to deal with them) than in those that had lower vulnerability. Usually, it is the developing countries in Africa, Asia and South America that bear the brunt of such events because of their geographic location and inadequate funding and infrastructure. Between 3.3 and 3.6 billion people live in these vulnerable areas. But now even the richer countries in the developed world such as Canada, the United States, and nations in Europe are getting a taste of floods, wildfires and hurricanes as they never did (and usually ignored) before, and people there are now running helter-skelter for shelter.

The rich developed countries promised $100 billion per year under the IPCC and Paris Agreement by 2020 to help developing nations to help mitigate climate change, but they have not kept that promise. Many countries do have pragmatic policies in place to fight climate change and global warming, but few have been implemented and many seem at cross-purposes with so-called development targets.

More money is still being pumped into fossil fuels and fossil fuel exploration by both the public and private sectors than is being earmarked for climate control and mitigation. Much more active citizen participation is required (we need to shout louder), both in terms of awareness and money spent, more research is needed and, of course, much more political support needs to be given so that alternatives can be explored and put into place. Big oil and big industry always say that they have to keep the interests of their stockholders and shareholders in mind, which is why they are hell-bent on maximizing profits (to hell with the environmental costs that might incur), but clean air, clean water, a comfortable temperature, availability of food are just as important, if not much more important, for the well-being of any stockholder or shareholder. You may hold stocks worth millions, but of what use are they if you are choking to death, being poisoned by what you eat or drink or are in imminent danger of being swept away in your Bentley by a flash flood or toasted to a crisp by a wildfire?

The retreating glaciers and ice sheets are another major cause of worry — they are leading to irreversible changes in the ecosystems of these areas. (Recently, as the ice sheets have melted earlier than usual with the advance of summer, king penguin chicks, still not ready in their waterproof outfits, have drowned en masse. Polar bears are starving to death and raiding garbage bins in Alaskan towns.) The poles are heating up at a faster rate than the rest of the planet, and that bodes ill, because they lock up most of the freshwater on the planet in ice. If this ice is allowed to melt, it will cause the monumental flooding of coastal lands.

At the rate we are going, it seems difficult to keep global warming below the target of an increase of 1.5 degrees Celsius in the twenty-first century. It is most likely going to exceed that figure; some say the increase might even be as much as 4 degrees Celsius.

Already around half the world's population suffers from extreme water scarcity for at least part of the year. In developing countries, women and young girls (who ought to be in school) have to walk for miles every day to fetch water from faraway wells. Fights regularly break out in urban areas when a water tanker finally arrives in the neighbourhood. All one needs to do, to realize how vital water is, is to turn off your taps for a single day and see how far you get in your daily activities.

All of the above seems as unpleasant and ugly as a gargantuan oil spill in the ocean, but thankfully, it's not all bad news. The IPCC has itself has claimed in Part 3 of its 'Summary for Policy Makers' that there are existing land management technologies and practices that can be winners in a few years even if they may need upfront investments. Land restoration and rehabilitation are key to this for the overall health and well-being of the planet and to mitigate climate change.

Besides, people and even countries and cities around the world are including adaptation in their climate policies and plans, even if these may not be equally distributed across the board and may be piecemeal. (Cities like Delhi have tried out the odd-even number plate scheme when pollution became a major threat and have banned petrol vehicles over ten years and diesel vehicles more than fifteen years old from plying on the roads. And now there's what they call a 'Graded Response Action Plan' (GRAP) that has been put into place to tackle air pollution stage by stage. Recently, the whole of London was declared an 'Ultra-Low Emission Zone', where motorists have to pay a surcharge every day that they use vehicles that do not meet emission standards.) Awareness is growing and, more importantly, children are being educated on how to deal with a world that we have mucked up good and proper and that they will inherit, and many are becoming loud, shrill and vehement whistleblowers with their justified outrage.

As mentioned earlier, many governments (sadly, including ours) don't like whistleblowers very much and will get after them in quick time and use heavy-handed means to stifle their warnings. And many governments (usually the same ones) love being gatekeepers, though sadly in this case they usually guard the wrong gates. But they do have to face up against thousands of institutions, non-governmental organizations (NGOs) and ordinary citizens around the world who are firmly guarding the right gates (against the exploitation of the environment for so-called 'development' and rip-off profiteering by conscience-less big businesses), often in the face of tremendous odds and opposition.

Wonderful Whistleblowers

There are thousands of NGOs around the world – national, international, regional and local – that have taken up cudgels for the cause of the environment, campaigning for clean air, clean water and, well, the bare necessities of life! Look around in your own neighbourhood, and you may find one just around the corner – as in fact I did, many years ago when I first shifted to Delhi. Many of these NGOs were started by just one or two determined, outraged and often outspoken young people (more often than not students), and then swelled to become country- and even world-wide institutions and movements. Also, there is media that has devoted itself to the cause through magazines (and now online) and remarkable documentaries on the subject. Of course, it is impossible to list all of them, but here are a few of the better- and lesser-known, as well as some remarkable individuals who have moved mountains through sheer persistence and hard work and networking. Some focus on specific areas and problems, such as ocean pollution, the protection of forests and other natural habitats or even of a single species of endangered animal. Others are more multidisciplinary. Several of these gatekeeping NGOs have been pounced upon on one pretext or another by governments (sadly, including our own) and have been bound and gagged because the people in power didn't like what they were pointing out. And sadly, this was often because it went against their own personal agendas. Having said that, there is always the outside chance that some of these NGOs are not quite what they make themselves out to be, so you need to have your ears and eyes open when you sign up to join them. Equally, there are government projects and institutions that actively promote environmental protection by aiding local people, NGOs and those interested by providing financing and know how and promoting tourism, so yes, governments can be good and very powerful gatekeepers too!

With apologies to those NGOs, institutions and people who justifiably think they ought to have been included here but have not (only due to prevent this book from swelling to over 2,000 pages, which would not be eco-friendly!), here are just a tiny few that function in India and abroad:

One of the best-known organizations worldwide is Greenpeace, whose often daring and unusual modes of protest have captured the public imagination. They have four campaigns: first, to stop climate change; second, to preserve the oceans; third, to promote sustainable agriculture and fourth, to prevent another nuclear catastrophe.

In the past, they have physically tried to stop whaling ships from harpooning whales (the harpoons are loaded with explosives) by riding in zodiacs around their ships. Greenpeace India has pointed out a nasty thing or two about our environmental policies, making the government set its wolves on them.

The Indian wing of Greenpeace got into trouble with the government and was basically shut down in 2014–15 for allegedly infringing upon the Foreign Contribution Regulation Act. This was after its earlier campaigns exposed mercury pollution, mining in forested areas and a scandal surrounding the dumping of waste by France in India in 2006. Its anti-nuclear, anti-thermal power stance and opposition to genetically modified crops made the Intelligence Bureau accuse it of being a threat to Indian economic security.

The World-Wide Fund for Nature (WWF) is another international NGO. Its India branch has its secretariat in New Delhi. It has been around for over fifty years, aiming to protect natural heritage and ecology. Climate change and energy conservation are particular areas of focus.

Chintan, based in New Delhi, has done remarkable work in promoting sustainable and equitable growth for every member of society (the IPCC has been pointing out that this is one major issue) through ensuring responsible and sustainable consumption, thus preventing waste (remember: 25–30 per cent of food goes waste!) and encouraging sensible consumption patterns, besides facilitating better waste management. Thankfully, we in India have a natural tendency to refurbish, reuse and recycle, rather than to bin things we have used. We call it jugaad! But now we're becoming wasteful too.

The Ashoka Trust for Research in Ecology and the Environment (ARTREE) is an environmental think-tank that has been globally recognized.

The Wildlife Trust of India focuses on dealing with India's wildlife crises, such as the human–animal conflict, which has been increasing manifold in recent years thanks to our incursions into and destruction of wild, natural habitats.

The Environment Trust's chief goal is to create innovative evidence-backed research solutions to environmental problems.

Navdanya was created in 1984 with a mission to promote biodiversity conservation, organic farming, seed-saving and farmers' rights.

FORREST hopes to strengthen the human–nature bond (which is being rapidly eroded nowadays) to promote peaceful co-existence. They work in habitat restoration, water conservation, education and awareness, biodiversity conservation, natural farming, waste management and composting.

Pune-based Kalpavriksh was founded in Delhi in the late seventies by students of Delhi University, in a campaign to protect Delhi's Ridge Forest. They were also among the first to blow the whistle on the controversial Narmada dam project, which later gave rise to the Narmada Bachao Andolan spearheaded by Medha Patkar.

It now focuses on networking, research, activism, environmental education and litigation.

The Bombay Natural History Society (BNHS), which came into being on 15 September 1883, is one of the largest NGOs in India and deals with conservation and biodiversity research. They had people like Dr Salim Ali and S Dillon Ripley at the helm. Dr Ali was chiefly responsible in getting the Keoladeo National Park notified as a bird sanctuary even as plans were being hatched to use the land for agriculture, and he ensured that the Silent Valley remained a safe haven.

The Centre for Science and Environment (CSE) is a Delhi-based think tank that was founded in 1980 by the late Anil Agarwal and is now run by Sunita Narain. Its ambit runs from investigation in food adulteration to consumer product safety. Every year, the centre brings out a State of India's Environment Report, published under the 'Down to Earth' moniker, which is the name of the fortnightly magazine they publish.

Many foreign-based NGOs are becoming extremely vocal and direct in their protests. At the forefront recently was the 'Just Stop Oil' group, whose members have taken to the controversial method of forming human chains and walking slowly down roads in major cities around the world. Their activities also include spraying paint on works of art in museums and interrupting sporting and musical events. These antics are naturally not making them very popular with the general public, who have to get to work or pick up children from school, and who have paid good money to see a match or performance, so it's debatable whether they're doing any good to their cause (which is calling an immediate halt to oil and gas exploration and extraction). They claim, sadly with some truth, that they can only draw attention to the cause by making a thorough nuisance (spectacle, some would say) of themselves. As in every field, there is rivalry and competition (often for grants and funding) even between NGOs, and they are not averse to pulling one another down. (Like the crabs in the bucket story!) All of them, one supposes, have their pros and cons, and you have to balance these out to reach any conclusion, especially if you want to sign up with them.

Awareness in the media has also grown manifold. Today, most major newspapers have environmental correspondents exclusively covering this beat, who tell us what hera pheri is going on and where. But, as with media worldwide, it is always sensible to check on the media organization's antecedents and credentials (who owns it or finances it and what its political leanings are) before accepting everything that it publishes as gospel. The same holds true of the broadcast media, which is often so much shriller and in-your-face than print. Where broadcast media often falters is in following up dramatic stories and exposes, so that you never really have closure on an issue. And this is mostly because some other dramatic (and usually political) story has just broken and must now hog the limelight!

There are some truly remarkable documentary filmmakers who have produced sometimes very controversial (and difficult to watch) films on the state of the environment and wildlife in our potpourri planet today and of our future prospects. Sir David Attenborough is a household name and a remarkable narrator who has brought out myriad stories from across the planet about the state of the environment and the loves and lives of so many of its denizens. Camera technology has improved by leaps and bounds and we are now making discoveries and getting insights into the most private aspects of animals' and plants' lives and behaviour and how climate change and global warming are affecting them.

One distressing aspect is that many respectable natural history television channels these days are focusing more on the blood and gore aspects of natural life: the bloody territorial battles between vengeful lion prides for example, or between males of various species over females – these are often battles to the death. The names of these series such as Animal Fight Club and Man vs Wild really says it all. And sometimes the stories are so pat that you wonder if the script was written after a whole lot of raw footage was shot and then cobbled together to construct the drama.

We have some very respectable environmental publications in India today: *Down To Earth* is published fortnightly from New Delhi and edited by Sunita Narain (of CSE mentioned earlier). It is one of the foremost of these publications and deals with the politics of environment and development. Back in the early eighties, there was a sudden influx of glossy wildlife-related magazines, most of which have folded up. But Bittu Sahgal's Sanctuary Asia (born 1981) and later Cub (born 1984), published from Mumbai, have stood firm. In 2000, 'Kids for Tigers', an educational outreach programme was launched to help children connect with nature by taking them on trails and hikes and through workshops, festivals and camps. In 2015, Sanctuary Asia expanded to become a non-profit foundation: the Sanctuary Nature Foundation.

There have been remarkable individuals too who have shaken and stirred up matters pertaining to the environment. Back in the 1960s, Rachel Carson brought out her seminal book *Silent Spring* on the disastrous impact of the pesticide DDT on the magnificent peregrine falcon, which nearly went extinct as a result. (The ingestion of the pesticide by the prey of the falcons led to the birds laying thin-walled eggs that broke rather than hatched.) The book resulted in a ban on the use of the pesticide in many countries (we have been slow to follow, and DDT is still being used in India), and brought out more awareness about how we are poisoning our planet and life on it by the indiscriminate use of these chemicals. Like most pesticides, DDT does not distinguish between a pest and a useful insect, and in any case, an insect usually only becomes a pest if the natural balance has been upset (usually by us).

Guardian Angels Going Strong

Various species too have had their special guardian angels: Jane Goodall was there for the chimpanzees (and discovered they could use tools), the late Dian Fossey (who was murdered, probably by poachers) for gorillas and Birute Galdikas for orangutans being three very famous ones. All of them started off armed with just grit, determination, interest and a quest for knowledge.

I am constantly amazed and considerably cheered-up when I read about field biologists who have devoted their entire working lives doggedly following (often obscure) animals, birds, insects, amphibians, fish, flora and ecosystems that have caught their imagination and sparked their curiosity.

Salim Ali ('the Birdman of India') got curious about the yellow splotch on a sparrow's breast, which set him off on a lifetime of documenting the birds of the Indian subcontinent and which resulted in his (and S. Dillon Ripley's) magnum opus, the *Handbook of the Birds of India and Pakistan.*

In 2018, Greta Thunberg, then just a fifteen-year-old schoolgirl and now a household name, sat outside the Swedish Parliament every Friday, urging it to do more for the mitigation of climate change. Her protests caught the imagination of students worldwide, leading to similar protests, and she stunned the attendees of the United Nations Climate Action Meeting in 2019 with her now iconic sledgehammer speech: 'You have stolen my dreams and my childhood with your empty words ... We are at the beginning of a mass extinction and all you can talk about is money and fairy tales of eternal economic growth. How dare you?'

We had some of the toughest wildlife protection laws in the world drafted in our Wildlife Protection Act of 1972 by Dr MK Ranjitsinhji and stalwarts like the late Kailash Sankhala, who was known as the 'Tiger Man of India' as the first director of Project Tiger.

The late Sunderlal Bahuguna began the famous 'Chipko' movement in the 1970s to protect forests in the Himalayas: Villagers spontaneously hugged trees in order to prevent their felling. His efforts convinced then Prime Minister Indira Gandhi to impose a

fifteen-year ban on the felling of green trees, but he fell out with later governments when he protested against the construction of the controversial Tehri Dam in Uttarakhand and was arrested.

But it would be foolish for us, and especially the government, to forget his slogan for the Chipko movement: 'Ecology is economy'.

The Bishnois of the deserts of Rajasthan are known for their fierce protection of wildlife and their environment; of the precious khejri tree that grows in the deserts. They have even chased down film stars they caught ostensibly poaching. The founder of this religious sect, Guru Jambeshwar, decreed back in 1485 that the cutting down of trees and killing of animals was forbidden. In 1780, the maharaja of Jodhpur, Ajay

Singh, ordered the felling of trees in the village of Khejari because he needed the wood for a new palace. A Bishnoi lady, Amrita Devi, was having none of it and, along with 362 others, stood around the trees, hugging them even as the maharaja's soldiers cut them to pieces. Appalled and ashamed, the maharaja stopped the felling. This was in fact the original 'chipko' movement, and the Bishnois have remained staunch protectors of their desert environment.

In her 2023 movingly lyrical book *Marginlands* (Picador India), Arati Kumar-Rao recounts the remarkable story of the creation of 'ice-stupas' in the dry cold desert of Ladakh by Ramon-Magsaysay winner and engineer Sonam Wangchuck. On 5 August 2010, the capital city Leh suddenly received a year's worth of rain in just two hours, causing havoc, and this was just for starters. Four equally if not more devastating floods between 2010 and 2018 indicated that extreme weather had arrived and was wreaking havoc on the agricultural schedule of the region. Normally, the spring crops were fed by snow meltwater, after which the glaciers took over, melting gently and keeping the valleys green and lush. But with a one-degree rise in temperature over the last forty years, the snowfall has become erratic and the glaciers are backing up the mountain, melting and releasing their water later in summer, leaving spring, a vital crop-growing period, high and dry.

In 2013, Wangchuk, while visiting villages near Leh, noticed a large lump of ice under a bridge, which had not yet melted, being shaded from the sun. Hmm... what if, what if he could create something like that artificially? The answer was simple, ingenious jugaad! He pumped water up tall pipes through a fine spray-nozzle at night, when the temperatures went down to minus 30 degrees Celsius. The spray, while falling back to earth, turned to ice, forming an upside-down cone around the pipe (rather like an ice cream cone, except that this one didn't have any chocolate cream!). And a cone exposes the least area to any sunlight, so the ice does not melt rapidly. The very first cone reached a height of six feet and contained 1,50,000 litres of water. After that, there was no looking back, as locals adopted the scheme enthusiastically. He's been thinking bigger: of creating an artificial glacier, which will auto-replenish itself every year.

But Wangchuk realizes that while this may be the solution to the problem in Ladakh, it doesn't tackle the root cause: global warming and climate change due to increasing fossil fuel use and over-consumption. For that, he has appealed to the world to reduce its carbon footprint, to consume less, travel wisely and not waste. Ladakhis, who have a very small carbon footprint compared to us city-dwellers, are paying the price for our sins and excesses.

There have been so many other illustrious figures, be they activists, scholars, fresh-faced students and ordinary people, who have taken up the cudgels for the cause as fiercely as Rottweilers guarding their patch, producing studies and reports and often coming down on the streets to protest. They have to face off against stonewalling bureaucracy, deliberately deaf ears, even threats to life, limb and freedom, raids and harassment by government enforcement agencies and arrests, not to mention the power behind big money and greedy vested interests.

Universities and research institutions around the world too are contributing their bit by publishing detailed and painstaking reports on the various aspects of the environment, be it climate change, global warming, the threat to wildlife and ecosystems and oceans or even an endangered species. Knowledge that really governments and people in power would do well not to ignore – in the end, we are all in the same boat, and if it sinks, so will they.

'Environmental studies' is now being taught in schools too, which is the right place to begin, because it is going to be these schoolchildren who are going to inherit the monumental garbage dump and its toxic contents and choking air that we leave behind and must learn how best to deal with them.

It's certainly not all only academic: we can and have made differences on the ground too. Back in 2002, the Delhi Development Authority (DDA) gave a large chunk of land (approximately 457 acres) adjoining the banks of the Yamuna River in Wazirabad, North Delhi, to the Centre for the Environmental Management of Degraded Ecosystems (CEMDE) of Delhi University to develop into a biodiversity park under the guidance of the redoubtable Prof. CR Babu, along with the boots-on-the-ground lead scientist Dr Faiyaz Khudsar. When I first visited the site in 2002, it frankly looked like a place one would test battle-tanks: it was a wasteland. The soil was bitterly saline, discouraging plant growth, and I don't remember seeing a single tree anywhere. The plan was to recreate here the sort of ecosystems prevailing along the Yamuna basin – a really tall order, it seemed. But the scientists plotted their strategy cunningly. First they put in plants that would naturally suck up the excess salinity from the soil. Once they had done the job, the scientists began planting indigenous species of grasses and shrubs. Two rain-fed waterbodies were created, a 'large' deep one and a winding, 'small' shallow one. And hey presto, within three years, the water bodies were being visited by large numbers of migratory ducks, apart from the local waterfowl and waders that nested there. Animals such as nilgai, wild boar and mongooses abounded. And the final jewel in the crown was the appearance of that top predator, the leopard, indicating that the circle of life had been successfully completed. (Alas, its presence raised such a ruckus among the local people – who lived cheek by jowl with the park – that ironically it had to be relocated.) They have various kinds of forest types and grasslands growing there, as well as a medicinal garden (which is like a natural pharmacy) and a butterfly park. It is also difficult to believe that you are in Delhi: it is cool, quiet, with just the breeze whispering through the tall wild grasses and yellow-footed green pigeons wheezing happily as they scoff up berries.

What was even more remarkable was how the park handled the 2023 Yamuna floods in Delhi. Because the floodplains in the area had been restored to their original state with their naturally occurring flora, the floods – all of 10 feet deep in the area – withdrew quickly without fuss, leaving no damage in their wake. This was in stark contrast with the much slower withdrawal and the trail of destruction the waters left downstream, where the floodplains had been ravaged by unauthorized construction.

Hard on the heels of the success of the Yamuna Biodiversity Park came the Aravalli Biodiversity Park in 2010, spread over around

380 acres, in a very different type of terrain and ecosystem, just on the border of Haryana. Now Delhi has seven such biodiversity parks. As I write this, across the border, in Haryana, the Aravallis have come under a shadow, as plans are being hatched to develop an insane, massive 'safari park' cum zoo for the area, which is to include the introduction of such animals as hippos!

Another lesson that came out of the biodiversity park experiment was that if you can keep the fingers of the government and bureaucracy out of the pie as far as possible and let the scientists get on with their work, they will produce the results. Now the biodiversity parks are being proudly shown-off to world leaders (by politicians and government officials no less!) about what has been achieved! Schoolchildren and university students regularly visit the parks, essential if they are to be made interested and assured that some good has been done on the ground.

But then again, on a recent visit to the park (in October 2023), I was shown a big, profusely illustrated book that had been brought out on all of Delhi's seven biodiversity parks. Simply and clearly, it showed how the parks had been developed, the flora and fauna to be found in them, the ecosystems that functioned there; it had before-and-after photographs, charts and diagrams and information on the natural cycle and how the food chain operated. It is a book that ought to be in every school and college library, not to mention government office and waiting room, and be mandatory reading. It showed what can and had been achieved – on the ground and in a throbbing metropolis like Delhi. And yet at the time of writing, they have not been given the go-ahead or the funds to publish and print it, which is really nothing short of gatekeeping at its worst and a criminal act.

India's first and only private wildlife sanctuary, the SAI (Save Animals Initiative), was created in Kodagu, Karnataka, by the late Anil Malhotra and his wife Pamela. They had wanted this since the time they were married and, then being based in the United States, tried to do so in Hawaii. But rampant tourism and development thwarted their plans. They then tried their luck in Uttarakhand, but here too things did not work out. So, they bought 55 acres of unused land in Kodagu from farmers who wanted to sell, and this figure gradually increased to 300 acres. The land had trees (and previously had been cardamom and coffee plantations) and a river running through it. The Malhotras had three rules: first, no tree would be cut; second, there would be no human interference and third, no poaching. The sanctuary now attracts tigers, leopards, elephants, dhole and a host of other animals and birds. Nature's regenerative powers combined with human determination, hard work and grit make an unbeatable combination. Another example of 'rewilding', albeit on a small scale.

A similar case is that of Jadav 'Molai' Payeng (the Forest Man of India) from Assam, who started off by planting bamboo saplings on sandbars in the Brahmaputra as part of a five-year project. After the term expired, Payeng continued planting more and looking after them. The 'Molai' forest today extends over more than 1,360 acres, consisting of thick jungle with tigers, rhinos and elephants and of course a wide variety of bird and plant life. Koli fisherwomen in Maharashtra (who normally are not permitted to operate boats) launched a campaign to popularize mangroves, so vital to coastal ecosystems, through tourism. They took on societal patriarchy, stuck to their guns and with the help (for a change) of the government, succeeded to the extent that all objections melted away.

Citizens living on the Baltic Sea began transplanting vital sea grass to areas that had been denuded of these (seagrasses form vital carbon banks, so important for controlling climate change), thus restoring the sea grass gardens.

In Montana, an oil and gas-producing state in the United States, a small group of youngsters sued their government for not considering climate change as a factor while approving fossil fuel projects. The judge ruled in their favour, maintaining that this was indeed unconstitutional, and the decision is being regarded as a hallmark one and sets a healthy precedent.

People in Ecuador have voted (in August 2023) to disallow oil drilling in a protected area of the Amazonian rainforest, which is home to at least two uncontacted local tribes. Gatekeeping at its best! So, we can make and have made a difference.

In the United States, the state of California has sued several of the world's giant oil companies for deception – in underplaying the risks posed by fossil fuels. The state has demanded compensation for future damages that may be caused. In fact, several states and municipalities have followed suit. At the time of writing, the oil companies have not responded. It seems similar to the manner in which the big tobacco firms refused to acknowledge that cigarette smoke caused cancer, despite the proof staring them in their faces. Sadly, down the ages and around the world, there have been many 'natural gatekeepers', whose knowledge, opinions, experience, attitudes, lifestyles and even lives we have rubbished, ignored and sometimes literally driven bulldozers over. For those sins of omission and our own of commission, we may sooner rather than later have to pay a very heavy price.

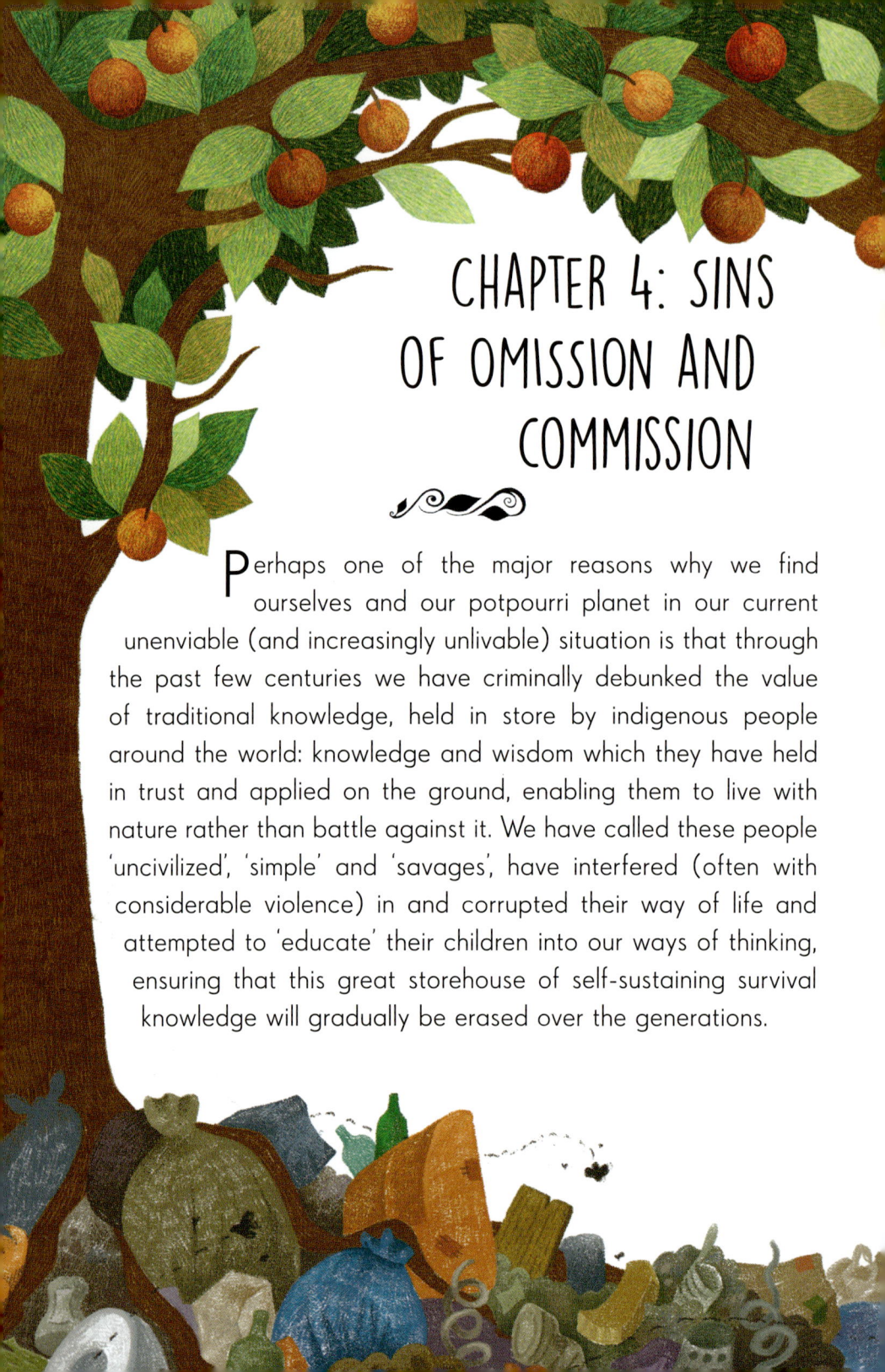

CHAPTER 4: SINS OF OMISSION AND COMMISSION

Perhaps one of the major reasons why we find ourselves and our potpourri planet in our current unenviable (and increasingly unlivable) situation is that through the past few centuries we have criminally debunked the value of traditional knowledge, held in store by indigenous people around the world: knowledge and wisdom which they have held in trust and applied on the ground, enabling them to live with nature rather than battle against it. We have called these people 'uncivilized', 'simple' and 'savages', have interfered (often with considerable violence) in and corrupted their way of life and attempted to 'educate' their children into our ways of thinking, ensuring that this great storehouse of self-sustaining survival knowledge will gradually be erased over the generations.

Knowledge Is Power

That knowledge could be vital to the
survival of our planet today because
it is based on one very simple underlying
principle: if you are directly dependent on nature
for your day-to-day life, for the food you eat, the
water you drink and the air you breathe, you will ensure that
you will not exhaust, destroy or pollute these natural resources or
their habitats. To put it bluntly, you do not pee and poop in your
glass of water or plate of dal-roti, or for that matter in anyone
else's, nor do you take all of the honey from a hive.

If you do not (as most of us living in cities and towns) see the
connection between the milk you drink and the cow that produces
that milk (many city-bred children are incredulous and sceptical
when they learn this), or the apple you bite into and the orchard
from which it comes from — you will not be so concerned. And
unfortunately, living in cities and towns divorces us from nature
and short-circuits that connection. Natural resources are pulled in
from the hinterland — be it wood, foodstuff, minerals and metals,
oil and gas — to be consumed in glittering, teeming cities. Nor do
we care about the mess we leave behind after extracting these

resources, or the pollution we cause while manufacturing all the things we want, or about the lives of the people living in those areas that we have completely destroyed by our activities.

Of course, modern technology is wonderful, but if it could be melded with traditional knowledge, which would imply working with nature rather than against it, it would really be a force to be reckoned with. For instance, if we would like to run a canal through a desert, it might be prudent to listen to what locals, who have been living in the area for eons, have to say about the geography of their landscape and of the lay of the land. They know not only where the water might lie beneath the sands, but how it gets refilled or percolates down after the rains, and in which direction the land slopes. It would be stupid to run a canal or build a road through an area blocking the natural flow of water, causing it to collect and stagnate on one side, rather than naturally let it run its course, and percolate into a well that has existed for thousands of years. We've done this and much worse all over the world (the much-touted Indira Gandhi Canal in Rajasthan is one example), time and time again, and one of the consequences of this is the trouble we're facing with global warming and climate change today.

Our sins of omission and commission have been many and varied, and it's high time we started making good and trying to repair the dreadful damage we have done. And that is what modern technology should be aiming its clever guns towards.

Our Own Worst Enemy and Bestie

For too long have we cast nature as the 'enemy', to be tamed and curtailed. Indigenous people the world over, be they our Adivasis, the Amazonian Indians, the Inuit, the Aborigines of Australia, the Native Americans, have a radically opposing attitude. In her incandescently furious book *Wild – An Elemental Journey* (Penguin, 2006), British writer and journalist Jay Griffiths expresses her 'rage against the hollow men, the stuffed shirts who are the agents of the wasteland, making the Amazon and the Arctic an overheated suburbia'. The world's forests she says have not only been stolen but have been badly misrepresented as being dark and doom-laden places, a viewpoint often endorsed in classical literature. A major attitudinal makeover is in order, and fortunately some writers and ecologists have recognized this: well-known environmentalist Vandana Shiva has said 'from the forests we learned democracy' (which now makes me wonder is that why we are now so keen to destroy our forests?!) Democracy begins with the acceptance that there are other points of view, other ways of knowing, other languages, that debate and discussion must happen, and forests, with their bewildering biodiversity, are a shining example of a functioning democracy. Rabindranath Tagore maintained that democratic pluralism and an ecological culture were hallmarks of Indian culture. How true that is in the present scenario is up for debate, or is it up for grabs too?!

For this change in attitude to arise we need to recognize that in spite of all our magical gadgets, glittering gizmos, and steel-and-glass lifestyles, we are still basically flesh-and-blood natural animals, again something that indigenous people the world over have recognized, accepted and lived by.

227

I will never forget the sheer exultation I felt on a walk I took on the Delhi Ridge with my rather crazy Labrador during a big, boom-bang thunderstorm and downpour that whipped the trees into a bendy-frenzy of dancing and pelted us with silver raindrops and hail that felt like airgun pellets, turning the narrow pathways into streaming torrents in no time at all. 'Lightning and thunder, will tear us asunder!' I yelled exultantly at the equally delighted dog as we splashed our way down the path. By the end of the walk, my eyes were probably as bright and sparky as those of the happy, wet dog, and my grin as wide as his! For all those 'stuffed shirts' and 'hollow men', I would seriously recommend a thorough dunking in a muddy pond crammed with beaming, booming raincoat yellow bullfrogs, puffing up their blue cheek-pouches like Satchmo, and wooing the ladies of their liking through hoarse croaky music!

It's not only a change in attitude that is needed: indigenous people do know how to manage their landscapes without destroying them. One guiding philosophy is never to take more than you can give. It was believed that the Amazonian rainforest was a pristine wild habitat, until it was discovered that it had been managed as a 'forest garden' by locals for at least the last 11,000 years! The soil of the Amazon rainforest is poor, so to muscle it up, the tribes created terra preta, a soil management system involving mud, biomass, charcoal, bones and manure.

Tellingly, Griffiths quotes one Yanomami Indian from Brazil as saying: 'We do not use the word "environment". That is your word for what you have left of what you have destroyed (*Wild: An Elemental Journey*, Penguin 2006). What has been destroyed until at least

2018 is 17 per cent of the Amazon rainforest, and if this figure reaches 20–25 per cent, it will tip into becoming a non-forest ecosystem consisting of degraded savannah.

Up in the Arctic, the Inuit (from Greenland and Canada) and Saami (from Scandinavia) have lived perfectly happily in their icy blue-and-white land, hunting whales and seals for food and to provide them with clothing, shelter and heating. Not an easy life for sure, but not a destructive one either, for they made sure they never hunted more than what they required. When the white man arrived, like a pestilence, as he did in so many other wild habitats around the world, all he saw in his ignorance was a wilderness, and proceeded to destroy the locals' way of life, corrupted their children's education and introduced the people to alcohol and drugs and the lethal diseases they carried. Those Arctic landscapes are today melting away rapidly thanks to global warming, and the Inuit's self-sustaining lifestyle has all but been destroyed. The Inuit called the white man 'Qallunaat', which has several meanings, including 'the people who change nature' – and this is not a compliment! A sculptor called Looty Pijamini bitterly complained to Griffiths, 'White people are like a disease. You came and took as much as you could, whales and muskox, and then after you'd hunted everything out, you tell us we're not allowed to hunt more!' I wonder if he realized how universally relevant his complaint was!

Global warming and climate change are shortening the winters more and more, causing the ice to thin earlier. This has caused some 3,000 Peary caribou to crash through and drown while on a migration route that had been used for a thousand years. Polar bears too need the ice in order to hunt seals; warmer winters are causing the ice to break up early and the roofs of their dens to crash down on cubs – or to scare them out into the open at a time when they are most vulnerable. Mosquitoes have turned up here for the first time ever. It's being predicted that there will be no summer ice left by 2070.

Playing God with Mother Nature

Water and gravity make for a combination as lethal as that of deuterium and tritium in a hydrogen bomb, and we mess with them at our peril. Yet, that's what we've been doing for decades, here and around the world, constructing massive dams that strangulate rivers in order to generate cheap hydro-power and to irrigate fields. Huge swathes of forest have been drowned for the cause – here in India, even in protected areas such as the Corbett National Park. And far too often we have not properly taken into account the consequences of our actions, which are now manifesting themselves in no mean fashion. You cannot garrot a mighty, wilful river, and not expect it at some time or the other to have an aneurysm. It will by hook or crook flow down to the sea in any way it can, by bulldozing through dams, expansively overflowing its banks (and taking down and drowning everything in its way) and piling silt on its bed so it rises and eventually just flows over a dam, barrage or any other obstruction. Our sacred Ganges and the mighty Brahmaputra are just two examples of such rivers which we have dammed and dredged and attempted to throttle, but which continue to have their way. And that has cost thousands of people living alongside them their lives, livelihoods, livestock, homes and crops.

With extreme rainfall events occurring more regularly than ever before, due to climate change, the rivers are losing their tempers much more frequently and much more violently. Worse, it's rare that the people so affected are ever properly compensated for the grief this has caused them, which is an error of both omission and commission.

Building enormous dams was once seen as a way to control floods, generate electricity (hydro-power), irrigate vast areas of land and to supply ever-thirsty and growing cities with an assured water supply. In India, we built more than 5,300 of them, with over 400 more in the pipeline. Delhi, for example, gets its water from the Tehri Dam, 300 kilometres away (against which Sunderlal Bahuguna had protested and been arrested). Also, it seemed cost-effective: the gains in terms of power generation, irrigation, etc., were far greater than the costs involved in building the dams.

But as mentioned above, what giant dams also did was to silt up rivers: sediment choked up behind the walls of the dams and in the reservoirs, causing the riverbed to rise and eventually overflow, after extreme rainfall events. Downstream, less sediment was deposited in the deltas, which was needed in order to compensate for that lost by erosion by the sea, causing them to sink. It's said that between 74 and 95 per cent of the sediment in major rivers such as the Mahanadi, Krishna and Narmada does not reach their deltas. Also, the presence of dams interferes with the migratory and breeding patterns of fish (such as the hilsa) and mammals such as the river dolphin. The Farrakha Barrage is said to be responsible for the nearly total disappearance of the hilsa, the fish so beloved of the hearts and tummies of the Bengalis, thus impoverishing the average family's dining table as well as the livelihood of the fisherfolk who depend on it.

The sediment and organic matter trapped behind the massive dam walls are not properly aerated and produce anoxic bacteria (that can live in low-oxygen environments) which emit methane rather than carbon dioxide. And methane is a far more powerful greenhouse gas. According to the National Institute for Space Research, Brazil, methane emissions from large dams are responsible for 30 per cent of the global methane emissions from anthropogenic sources. Ten per cent of the of dams emit more greenhouse gases than conventional fossil-fuel-gas-powered plants of the same capacity. The situation is exacerbated in tropical countries like India, where higher temperatures lead to even higher methane emissions.

That apart, big dams can cause seismic rumbles due to the weight of the water held back in the reservoirs, especially in seismically sensitive areas as the Himalayas, besides resulting in the wholesale destruction of biodiversity and the felling of forests that occur when they are built. (The Kalagarh Dam in Corbett drowned prime forest areas). Humanitarian costs too are incalculable: invariably tens of thousands of usually very poor, landless people, often tribals and Adivasis, are displaced without adequate compensation given for the loss of land (if they owned any) or livelihood. The Adivasis, for example, comprise just 8 per cent of the population yet make up 59 per cent of the over 11.5 lakh people displaced by twenty large dams during the 1990s. This human cost never enters the calculations when such projects are being planned. We are the third largest big dam builders in the world (after the United States and China). Today in several countries large dams are being decommissioned. But we're planning twenty-six new huge dams in the Northeast, attempting to garrot the mighty Brahmaputra.

Alternatives to this approach have been suggested: these could include a network of interconnected small tanks and canals (as existed in the times of yore), a series of small dams and the harvesting of rainwater — as put out by The South Asia Network on Dams, Rivers and People.

Dykes and embankments do much the same thing: attempt to constrain what cannot be constrained.

Apart from that they separate the river from its floodplain and other wetlands into which any excess water during flooding can not only take refuge but also enrichen the soil with silt. Walk along the banks of a river which are flanked by sloping cement walls (like the Sabarmati at Ahmedabad) and you cannot but feel uneasy: if there is a cloudburst and the river rises over, disaster will strike. Had there been a marsh or swamp, with waving wild grass along the banks of the river, you would not have felt so discomfited; the excess water would have been sponged up.

It might be prudent to make it mandatory for politicians, planners and engineers involved in such schemes and grandiose projects to spend the three monsoon months camped beside one such throttled torrent, or creaking dam, and observe what happens before they start blasting and building. A river or mountain stream in spate is a terrifying spectacle, as has been clearly demonstrated in our hill states recently. Entire villages, buildings, bridges, temples and roads have been scornfully tossed aside like so much flotsam and jetsam by the furious roaring waters, and yet we want to choke them more!

To top it all we are now contemplating schemes to link major rivers together, ostensibly for irrigation purposes. With their heads in the clouds, proponents of this scheme want to interconnect all of India's major rivers into one massive network. This, they say, will prevent floods, irrigate vast areas and supply water to cities and industries, and even perhaps challenge the railways and roadways in transportation. They say it will prevent 'wasted' water from flowing into the sea. The National River Linking

Project sets its sights on linking sixteen rivers in peninsular India and fourteen emanating from the Himalayas. Thus, for example, the Godavari and Krishna will link up and the Ganges, Damodar and Subarnarekha will join hands too. Thirty canals, over 1,500 km, and 3,000 dams and reservoirs will contribute to the massive network. The Ken-Betwa link — a project given the go-ahead and costing 45,000 crore — aims to take water from the Ken River to the Betwa, both flowing through Madhya Pradesh and Uttar Pradesh, via a 320-kilometre-long canal. Incidentally it will involve the drowning and felling of vast tracts of prime forest and scalping of the Panna National Park into two — where you could go to jail for seven years if you accidentally ran over a partridge or peafowl.

You can imagine problems that can and probably will, arise with such schemes: there will be massive hydrological issues, there will be issues of ownership between the states the rivers flow through (whose 'property' is it?) and there will be ecological issues. The water flowing down to the deltas and seas is not wasted: it carries silt which, as we have seen, is essential to buffer up the deltas (and prevent them from going under), and providing rich fertile soil for agriculture en route. And rivers, as we have seen, often have a will of their own. Also, every river has its own unique ecosystem, sustaining its own spectrum of species (sometimes endemic) of animals, birds, fishes, reptiles and amphibians, and mixing these with those of another river, far away, is like arranging a very unsuitable marriage match.

Again, the money could perhaps be better spent on many smaller-scale projects for the retention and maintenance of water bodies and the creation of small-scale dams and barrages spread across the country, especially in places where they are most needed.

As ever, those making these grand decisions will be far away from those who might have to face the consequences. In Mumbai, the eight-lane coastal road that has been built to ease the city's chronic traffic problems has destroyed its protective barrier against the sea — its mangroves — as well as played havoc with the livelihoods of the local Koli fisherfolk, who were the earliest residents of the city. Mumbai, largely reclaimed from the Arabian Sea, is set lower than the high tide mark, so when it rains and the tide comes in, its antiquated hundred-year-old stormwater drains can only surrender and let sea water in rather than the rainwater out! As children even back in the 1970s, we would pray that downpours would coincide with high tides, so the roads would be flooded and school would be closed (or we'd have a wonderfully splashy time trying to get to school!).

But Mumbai, tied with Los Angeles, is the second-most threated city in the world (Guangzhou is the first) when it comes to rising sea levels. Billions of dollars could be lost in damages if steps are not taken to mitigate the impact. The destruction of the protective shield of mangroves exposes the city even more to the raging invasive tides — besides ruining the habitat of Mumbai's legendary flocks of greater flamingo. The unprecedented twenty-four-hour cloudburst on 26 July 2005, when over 1 metre of rain drowned the city, cost 1,000 lives, and in the following ten years floods due to extreme rain-events have cost 3,000 more lives and $2 billion in infrastructure losses.

Down south, in Kerala, which has a turbulent coast, over forty rivers flow into the Arabian Sea from the Western Ghats, many of which have been blocked by dams or diverted through canals, preventing the sediment they carry from building up on the beaches as they sprawl into the sea. Ocean currents, running south to north (during the non-monsoon months) and north to south (in the monsoons) along the coast are the only way the sea can build up a beach. The government has built seawalls jutting straight into the sea, perpendicular to the coast, which during the non-monsoon months block the currents, piling up the sediment on the southern side of the wall and preventing it from building up on the beaches on the northern side. When the monsoons arrive, the tides on these enervated beaches rush right inland — causing devastating erosion in coastal villages.

There's a telling line from an old Bob Dylan ballad, 'Boots of Spanish Leather', which just coincidentally (and with no relevance to the context of the song) spells out the message stridently: 'Take heed, take heed, of western ways/ take heed of stormy weather…'

Yes, we still need to take heed of Western ways in many spheres of activity (over-consumption and waste, for example) but they are thankfully just beginning to become wise too, as people there get impacted themselves. And so must we — and even more urgently, because we're really first in the firing line of a lot stormier weather ahead if we do not.

CHAPTER 5:
LOCKING DOWN CARBON

Carbon dioxide (in cahoots with water vapor, and with its more dangerous sidekick methane and company) is the villain of the piece in regard to global warming and climate change, and we are allowing it to billow out into the atmosphere in increasingly gargantuan amounts. It is thus obvious that the gas has to be corralled, bound and gagged, as it were, so it can be rendered harmless. Whenever anything containing any form of carbon is burned (which means pretty much everything) it releases carbon dioxide — and usually a whole lot of other toxic colleagues. So, to protect our potpourri planet from overheating (and choking) we need to do two things: to 'set free' as little carbon dioxide into the air as possible every year, which is sadly not really happening. And, secondly, we have no choice but to try and capture some of the escaped carbon dioxide and imprison it in any way and any place we can.

In nature this is already happening — all the time — through the process of photosynthesis. Plants take in carbon dioxide, use it to grow and, when they die, bury it deep within the earth's surface, over the millennia turning the dead leaves, and organic matter it into coal, oil and gas. This, we discovered to our great delight, were excellent fuels, so we went and set free the locked-up carbon in these substances, by burning colossal amounts of these fuels and releasing carbon dioxide back into the air. Of course, we've now realized that this general amnesty has backfired, that there's far too much carbon dioxide around. Now, the only way out is to 'capture' or (this sounds more impressive) 'sequester' some of that escaped carbon, so that there's less of it muffling, heating up and choking our planet. That is what carbon sequestering is all about. We have to lock down excess carbon and store it away safely in 'carbon pools' or 'carbon sinks' preferably for as long as possible — hundreds to millions of years, if possible. As usual, different institutions and organizations have slightly differing definitions of what carbon sequestering is.

The United States Geological Survey defines it thus: 'carbon sequestering is the process of capturing and storing atmospheric carbon dioxide.'

The IPCC calls carbon capture and storage (CCS) basically the same thing, as 'processes in which a relatively pure stream of carbon dioxide from industrial sources is separated, treated and transported to a long-term storage location'.

Whatever. The fact remains that carbon dioxide, like a convict on the run, has to be captured and locked up for as long as possible!

Catch that Carbon – Then Let It Go!

We can and are doing this in two ways: by helping Mother Nature do what she's been doing since time immemorial and by using artificial, technological means. Most natural ecosystems, such as forests, grasslands, savannahs, marshes, peatlands, bogs, oceans, seagrass and seaweed meadows, mangroves, et al. lock down vast amounts of carbon, usually quite safely. But then we came around and messed up: we cut down or burned the forests, drained the marshes, cleared the grasslands to grow crops requiring fertilizers and pesticides, destroyed the mangroves, besides, of course, pumping out and mining vast quantities of oil, gas and coal.

Now we are trying to redress the balance by afforestation and reforestation programs: planting millions of trees on devastated wastelands, or in areas where forests once existed. They say we have space on earth for planting between 1 and 2 trillion trees more, which could 'sequester' some 205 billion tonnes of carbon dioxide. Even using wood for building and furniture (of course) will do, because wood sequesters one hell of a lot of carbon (which is why it burns so well). But it goes without saying that one of our chief priorities must be first to conserve these natural ecosystems so that they continue doing what they already are so efficiently. So, do not cut down huge swathes of forest, rip up the ocean beds and drain the wetlands and destroy the mangroves in the first place.

But even so, there are chinks in the armour in 'natural sequestration'. In fact, forests and grasslands are called 'volatile carbon sinks' because they can hold sequestered carbon for only so long: they are combustible, and thanks to global warming, forest and grassland fires have been roaring fast and furiously all over the planet, letting out all their locked-up carbon again in the form of carbon dioxide as well as other greenhouse gases. Then they may release carbon dioxide through decay. It's a nasty sort of vicious circle. And as mentioned before, there's us with our chainsaws and dredgers. But we can and are 'reforesting' areas so decimated by fire or destroyed by mining, either letting them grow back or planting them all over again.

Deforestation of course, is not a good idea per se: apart from exposing the soil to erosion and depleting it of nutrients, there's the mass carnage of biodiversity — the plants and animals and insects that lived there — and every living creature has a role to play in running the planet. We usually indulge in this mass massacre for agricultural purposes, to grow crops and raise plantations, or for creating feeding grounds for livestock, or mining and drilling for minerals, metals and oil and gas. But once the soil is depleted, and we attempt to reforest it, its ability to sequester is never as good, as was that of the original forest.

Unfortunately, we're still gung-ho about deforestation: clearing forests at will, replacing them with plantations. For example, the government wants to raise 370,000 hectares of palm oil plantations in Assam, a rich biodiverse region, at the cost of its invaluable rainforests and unique and often endemic flora and fauna. Palm oil plants have rapacious demands from the soil and need a lot of water.

Then there's always the risk of a political dispensation which equates development with the invasion of and felling of forests — as we saw not so long ago in Brazil (the approach has thankfully changed now!), and which sadly India appears heading straight towards, with the recent amendments to the Forest Act.

Even city or urban forests can sequester large amounts of carbon and so must be planned and planted. In addition to the carbon they suck up (and cities emit large amounts of carbon dioxide), they also lower the temperatures of both the place as well as its inhabitants.

It is hugely important to conserve and restore wetlands in order to mitigate climate change. Wetlands, such as marshes, sea coasts, seagrasses, mangroves and salt marshes sequester large amounts of carbon. As much as 20–30 per cent of the world's soil carbon is locked up in wetlands, which comprise only 5–8 per cent of the world's surface. Damaged or

destroyed wetlands must be restored (and there are many restoration projects being carried out around the world). Apart from acting as carbon sinks, they purify and enrich the water quality through filtration and preserve biodiversity.

But they are sensitive ecosystems and if disturbed can release the carbon stored in their plants and sediments back into the atmosphere. Thanks to global warming, wetlands, especially in the regions of permafrost, release oxygen and water into the soil on which bacteria act, and release large amounts of carbon dioxide into the atmosphere: turning the wetland into a carbon source rather than sink. Wetlands do naturally release methane too, and it's still unclear how they manage to store carbon while doing so.

Peatlands, which have suffered considerably at our hands, are said to hold around 30 per cent of the carbon in our ecosystem. But we have systematically drained them for agriculture and to build upon, causing gargantuan amounts of carbon to decompose and be emitted as carbon dioxide. Peatbogs lock up carbon in their partially decaying biomass, which, if allowed to decay completely, releases carbon dioxide, again turning them from saviour to sinner!

Of course, we need agriculture to feed ourselves, but the fields on which crops are grown score lower as far as the amount of soil organic carbon they store. They lose between 30–40 per cent of the carbon they hold in the form of plant material due to harvesting. We can reduce this loss by natural means, such as leaving harvested residues in the fields (though yes, often farmers have to clear their fields to sow the following crop), using manure as fertilizer, rotating crops and including perennial crops in the mix. It's thought that globally, soils contain more than 8,580 gigatonnes of organic carbon, more than ten times as that in vegetation.

Rising global temperatures can lead to algae blooms in soil microbes, causing the release of carbon dioxide. Organic farming (though considered not very profitable or popular at the moment), and the use of earthworms are of immense value too. Terra petra, human-made soil, contains a high content of biochar – which has a high amount of carbon, which is permanently locked up in this form.

Artificial sequestration of carbon really indicates how desperate we are to capture and lock down excess carbon dioxide. It means we lock up and store carbon in what one could say are underground safety vaults: these could be depleted oil and gas reservoirs, coalbeds too deep to be mined or saline formations. The carbon dioxide, say from an industrial plant, is actually compressed and piped to the place where it is to be imprisoned and then injected into these vaults – which may be one kilometre underground – where it can be safely stored for hundreds to millions of years. Basically, it's been locked away and we've thrown away the key! The carbon dioxide may be in a semi-fluid state, or may be dissolved in groundwater (brine, or soda water) and may even react with the minerals present to form solid carbon salts. This happens naturally too, and is what causes the formation of limestone. Limestone, thus created over billions of years, contains a lot of the earth's carbon.

We can and are trying to sequester carbon in the oceans too. The oceans naturally sequester carbon by what has been called the 'solubility pump'. Carbon dioxide on the ocean's surface reacts with and dissolves in water, and with the help of photosynthesis, seaweeds and marine algae convert this into organic carbon, which is stored in the ocean.

So, naturally seaweed and algae farming are the way to go! Seaweed grows in shallow, coastal seas and traps one hell of a lot of carbon, which is moved down deep into the ocean bed in the form of dissolved particles of organic matter. Here, it remains safely locked away for an eternity. There's a bonus too! Seaweed is quick-growing and can be harvested and safely converted (through a process called anaerobic digestion) to biomethane, which is a renewable natural gas.

One startling study maintained that if seaweed farms covered 9 percent of the earth's oceans, they could generate enough biomethane to supply the earth's equivalent demand for fossil fuel energy, remove 53 gigatonnes of carbon dioxide from the air and provide 200 kilograms of fish per head for 10 billion people! Talk about a win-win situation!

The 'wonder plant' of the ocean of course is marine phytoplankton, of which algae is a type. Marine phytoplankton is responsible for half of the global photosynthetic carbon fixation and produces half of the earth's oxygen, in spite of consisting of around just 1 per cent of the earth's biomass.

Seaweed farming is being carried out — especially in the Pacific and Indian ocean coastal regions, but really has to catch on: the IPCC has encouraged 'further research and attention' in this area.

The Bizarre Carbon Bazaar

In the world today, virtually everything can be bought or sold: property, automobiles, even governments and the hearts and minds of people too. And carbon is no exception! Nations and organizations around the world have set up a system by which if you, as a nation or industry or even individual, emit less carbon dioxide, you earn bonus points (in terms of dollars) and if you emit more you get minus points and may have to pay fines or more taxes. The final aim of this exercise is to render the earth 'net carbon-zero', which is to say the amount of carbon dioxide being emitted through our activities around the world should be equal to the amount of carbon dioxide being sequestered, or prevented from being emitted, in that period, so there is no net increase in the amount of carbon dioxide and other greenhouse gases in the atmosphere. We in India have set a target of becoming 'net zero' by 2070. Yes, it is a tall order, considering our current profligate habits and disinclination to change them!

Credits Vs Debits

Here, the concepts of 'carbon offsets' and 'carbon credits' come into play. A 'carbon offset' means you have reduced the amount of carbon dioxide you have emitted in one particular sphere of activity — say in an industrial plant — by a certain amount, which can equally compensate for an increase in carbon emissions in another sphere of activity — say transport — by the same amount.

A carbon credit which has to be bought at a price usually from a government or institution allows you to emit one tonne of carbon dioxide and the number of carbon credits you are allowed depend on emission targets that have been set. The valuation of carbon offsets and carbon credits is defined financially — in terms of dollars! And this is exchangeable and barterable between firms, countries and even individuals.

Formally they have been defined thus: a carbon offset is a reduction or removal of emissions of carbon dioxide or other greenhouse gases, made in order to compensate for emission made elsewhere. A carbon credit or offset credit is a transferable instrument certified by governments or independent certification bodies to represent an emission reduction of one metric tonne of carbon dioxide or greenhouse gases.

It was all kicked off back in 1977 when the United States Clean Air Act set up this bazaar. It allowed one facility to increase its emissions, provided it paid another facility to reduce its emissions (of the same pollutant) by a greater amount at its own facilities. In 1997 the United Nations kind of adjusted this scheme and bumped it up to nation-level, through its Clean Development Mechanism. Now, say country 'A' (usually a developed country) could pay country 'B' (usually a developing country) a sum of money to help the latter reduce its emissions through various programmes, and then claim the same emissions to help them meet their own emission targets, which would be reducing year on year. If country 'A' helped (meaning paid) country 'B' to reduce its emissions by say 100 gigatonnes worth of carbon dioxide through implementation of various programs, it would have that 100 gigatonnes worth of emissions to its credit, which would help it meet its own emission targets, which it otherwise would not have. These targets were set by the Kyoto Protocol of 1997 and the Paris Agreement of 2015, to which all but six countries agreed. (Famously, the United States pulled out when Donald Trump became president, but has rejoined since.)

Now as the idea of the whole exercise is to reduce the amount of carbon dioxide and other greenhouse gases being emitted, emission targets are set by countries and international organizations and are naturally being reduced, with the ultimate goal of achieving 'net zero'. Carbon credits are issued by national and international governmental organizations, which fix the number of credits that can be issued or bought, depending on emission targets that have been set. These emission targets are set by regulators and the number of credits allowed are limited and serve as a 'cap' — these are gradually reduced every year.

It's been suggested that carbon credits be thought of as a kind of 'permission slip' which allows you to emit a certain amount of carbon dioxide and other greenhouse gases every year, and that number reduces year by year. You have to mandatorily stay under that amount (the cap) or else face fines and penalties.

If you reduce the amount of carbon dioxide et al. you emit every year, you can issue carbon offsets. A company that produces less carbon dioxide than the number of credits it is allotted (by being energy efficient or using the latest technology) thus has a surplus. A company that emits more carbon dioxide than its credit allotment (say because it uses outdated technology) can buy credits from the surplus companies and so avoid paying fines and extra taxes which otherwise might be imposed on it while also respecting the cap.

Then there's the voluntary market, where companies and individuals want to reduce their emissions and earn carbon offsets simply because they want to: they are environmentally conscious perhaps, because their staff is thinking about the future of their children and grandchildren. There is nothing mandated here, it's all voluntary. A company may on its own decide to reduce its carbon emissions by so many thousand tonnes every year and work towards that noble goal and so earn carbon offsets. But the claims of such companies (and even individuals) have to be independently validated: that their activities did indeed lead to a reduction in the amount of carbon dioxide they emitted and that the claims were not just all hot air!

In 2020 the voluntary market was thought to be worth $400 million, and is expected to hit $10–25 billion by 2030, which is still less than what would be required if the earth is to meet its emission targets as set out by the Paris Agreement. According to one source, the global compliance market size in 2020 was $261 billion, translating into 10.3 gigatonnes of carbon dioxide equivalent being bought and sold that year.

Hera-Pheri and Horse Trading!

But there is apparently a lot of hera pheri going on in the voluntary market in India as a report from the CSE published in *Down to Earth* recently pointed out. The way I like to look at it is like this: on the one hand you have the winners: those institutions, organizations and good people, who emit less carbon than what they're allowed to do so. I like to think as every unit of carbon saved (say one-tonne carbon dioxide equivalent) as one unit of blessing. On the other hand, you have institutions, individuals and organizations that emit more carbon than they are allotted: these are the sinners and every unit of carbon above the limit, I count as one sin.

Now in the system, the blessees or 'winners' can sell their extra blessings to the sinners, who can absolve and offset their sins because of the blessings they buy! Of course, a third party has to come into play; the one who brings the winners and sinners together. They also decide how much each blessing or sin is worth and how many blessings accrue from the project – a figure that can be inflated and exaggerated.

This third party also helps potential winners to become full-time winners, through launching schemes and projects such as distributing fuel-efficient cookstoves, or encouraging plantations. They'll sell these smokeless chulas at subsidized rates to villagers, or help a farmer raise a plantation by providing them with saplings, and put a price on each 'blessing' that each chula or plantation generates: i.e., the amount of carbon emissions it saves say every year through being efficient and green. But more often than not, these third parties do not inform the end-users – the villagers or farmers – of the fact that their smokeless chulas are emitting blessings which really, they should be entitled to cashing in on, if not fully, at least to a proportion! Also, these third parties usually overestimate the number of blessings (carbon offsets) that these chulas generate, because they calculate the figures on the basis that they are being used every day of the year, whereas villagers (many who have either piped gas or LPG cylinders) say they use them very infrequently and only for boiling milk and water, and that it is impossible to cook for a family of seven or eight people on them! In cases where the villagers are informed of the 'blessings' emanating from their chulas, they are made to sign undertakings that they are not entitled to cashing in on them – and carbon offsets become the property of the third party! There is an ironical twist to this story: in many cases the villagers have found these fuel-efficient, less-polluting chulas not as efficient as they would like and, to improve their performance, in addition to the firewood, feed them with plastic waste, which emits even more, and very toxic, smoke! It is the age-old story of taking advantage of illiteracy and lack of awareness of one's rights. There are meant to be regulators and auditors to ensure a fair deal, but these are often as cagey and hush-hush as the third-party organizations.

In the case of plantations, it's much the same story. The farmers get their saplings — and know-how — either free or at subsidized rates, but they are told nothing about the blessings ensuing from these (or are made to forsake them), which the institutions cash in on. And the farmers then have to put in the toil and trouble to ensure that the saplings survive and grow. Bottom line: the end-users are being ripped off of the carbon credits that they should certainly be made aware of and perhaps be entitled to. The other basic issue is that this horse-trading enables rich polluters (such as oil giants) to continue polluting because they can afford to buy carbon offsets from those who pollute below their limits.

Carbon footprint is another term that is being freely bandied about these days. Basically, it's the amount of carbon dioxide and greenhouse gases we (individuals, companies, countries) emit through our everyday activities. This could include transport and electricity, the carbon dioxide emitted in the manufacture of things we buy and in heating and cooling homes. Thanks to their much higher consumption patterns people in the developed world usually have a much bigger carbon footprint than those in the developing world. According to the Carbon Dioxide Information Analysis Centre and the United Nations Development Programme, the average resident of the United States has a carbon footprint of 20.6 metric tonnes of carbon dioxide equivalent, which is five to seven times the global average. In 2021 our average global footprint was 1.9 metric tonnes. Lest we get smug at this point, we need to know that India is the third largest emitter of carbon dioxide (after the United States and China) and like everyone else on earth we have to do our bit in sucking back and locking down the genie we have all let out of the bottle.

PART III

Making Mama Nature Happy Again

CHAPTER 1: ARMAGEDDON OR GARDEN OF EDEN?

So, are we heading for Armageddon or will we be able to turn our precious planet into a garden of Eden? Hopefully we can avoid the first, but achieving the second is very unlikely. There are many who believe that what we've done is like letting a bulldozer run downhill without brakes — it is going to flatten everything in its way and destroy itself when it hits the bottom. There are others that think it may still not be too late, that we might be able to salvage the situation. There are also those (some of who hold positions of immense power) who do not believe there is any problem at all; that we should continue doing what we're doing, gassing away ad-infinitum; that the melting of the icecaps is a figment of the imagination; that one year's rain falling in four hours is par for the course and that 50 degrees Celsius is cool man, so good for your tan, but whew, where's the nearest air conditioner?! Then, there are those who say one thing (that they're all for protection of the environment, the reduction of greenhouse gas emissions and preservation of forests, blah-blah-blah) and do quite the opposite (diluting protection laws, increasing mining for coal and drilling for oil, opening up wildernesses for exploitation and decimating more of the rainforests). These may be the most dangerous of them all.

At the other end of the spectrum there are those (and around the world they're growing in number and decibels by the day) who insist that we must stop using and drilling for fossil fuels, right now, this instant! That we should go wholesale into renewable energy, consume less, eat less meat and drink less milk. That it is no longer a matter of choice, but one of survival.

Well, let's take a look at what we've been doing to try and prevent our potpourri planet from turning into a blast furnace in the near future and what more we need to do. One rather ironic sign that we're at last taking things seriously is that climate change and global warming are mentioned in headline news in nearly every single bulletin – and the media is notorious for its fickle memory. In fact, in the time it's taken to write this book, there's been one climate disaster after another in such quick succession that it's been hard to keep up!

But Mother Nature is now tapping us on our shoulders to remind us every so often: this is not a story that is going to get over anytime soon, and if we know what is good for us, we'd better start tackling the problem at a much more intense level. That tap on the shoulder could be an unseasonable hurricane, monsoons playing AWOL, cities choking and shutting down under smog, rapidly retreating ice sheets, seas rushing in... the list goes on. And in response we tighten emission controls, pledge vast amounts towards carbon capture and renewable energy, exhort societies to consume and waste less – basically making all the right noises. How much these resolutions have an effect on the ground is the point that is hotly debated.

Wanted! Tidal Wave of Protest!

One thing is for sure. Unless there is a vast groundswell of protest from people around the world, especially those living in democratic countries, the leaders and politicians are not going to move their butts to put into place tough legislation (to rein in polluting industries, for example), forget about implementing those laws. Yes, in many countries governments do make strict laws – even if people protest against them – but then they often fail to implement them thoroughly. Look at what happened to the laws banning plastic bags and bottles! They're still everywhere! Happily, groundswell support is increasing, but much too slowly. I sometimes wonder what might have happened if the terrible Libyan flood of 2023 (which is said to have swept away 20,000 people, overnight), or the Sikkim lake-burst or any suchlike disaster had occurred in any glittering metropolis in the United States or any developed nation. The furore would have gone ballistic!

To my mind, that groundswell of support is going to have to demand this first and foremost from its leaders: that this is one area where all the countries of the world, no matter what their ideals, religions or beliefs are, will just have to come together to tackle this issue. You could be red, black, blue, white, yellow, pink or green, it doesn't matter: you and your family will broil, burn, drown, suffocate, or be taken down by an avalanche, cyclone, hurricane, landslide or mudslide, sooner or later, no matter where you live, be it in swanky Santa Barbara in California or in a slum in Bangladesh. Not just you, but thousands and millions of people and families just like you. For every single one of us and for every single country on earth, this needs to become number one priority. We have to focus, and work on this issue as speedily, ferociously, unitedly and diligently as the scientists who sent Chandrayaan-3 to the moon did, or those scientists did in finding a vaccine for Covid. Like it or not, it has to become our raison d'etre. As Rachel Carson said, 'Man is a part of nature, and his war against nature is a war against himself' (*Silent Spring*, Houghton Mifflin 1962). We have to stop that war.

I like to think of it as though we're watching a meteorite heading straight for us – slowly at first, but rapidly gaining velocity as it draws closer. And we're still too busy squabbling amongst ourselves to either (a) take a good look at it, or (b) to unite and do something to stop it and send it back into deep space!

We've already seen some of the steps being taken to control the emissions of carbon and greenhouse gases: there's carbon capture (and all the commercial juggling we've created around it), there are massive clean-up drives on beaches and rivers, there are frozen zoos and seed banks, there are solar-, wind- and hydro-power generating plants, there are stricter pollution norms and caps on emissions, there is afforestation and reforestation and organic agriculture and there is captive breeding of endangered species, among others.

The Times Will Have to Be Changing!

And then there are our personal habits! The one thing that a lot of us will have to do is to consume and be satisfied with less (which alas flies in the face of the guiding light of a consumer society: shop till you drop!): shop sensibly and preferably self-sustainably, and absolutely do not waste. It's like that old saying: it's best to stop eating before you are full up, and I would like to add, choose what you want to eat sensibly. This means that Americans and Europeans will have to consume more sensibly, so that those in impoverished countries get to consume at least enough to be able to sleep without grumbling tummies. The earth simply does not have the resources to sustain a wasteful standard of living. It means that the developed countries need to waste far less, and that the developing countries shouldn't follow the example they have set so far. Recycling, reusing, repairing and refiguring should be the order of the day, something that Indians are already good at. A second look at the old more self-sustaining technologies – in construction and agriculture for example – and more importantly melding those old ways with modern technology could offer a way out. That brash new kid on the block, artificial intelligence, could play a role in this, using its 'brains' to optimize the use of resources in the most efficient, non-polluting and least wasteful manner possible.

There have been dark and dire predictions galore, often backed up by frightening statistics trotted out by scientists, researchers, journalists and writers who have dedicated lifetimes to their subjects. You don't even need these figures to realize what could happen if we do not radically change our way of thinking. In

India, our goal is 'development' so that we can catch up with the developed world. Of course, everyone in India (or a vast majority at least) would want to own a car, preferably an SUV — and why not? But if there are some 1+ billion cars running amuck on the roads, can you imagine the environmental carnage (excuse the pun!) that would occur in terms of the fossil fuels required, the pollution they would cause, the infrastructure required in terms of roads (again at the cost of the environment) and the sheer parking spaces they would need, to say nothing of the lakhs of lives lost because we drive like morons? And the alternative is there: fast, smooth, cool, efficient, door-to-door public transport. That needs to be booted up and how!

What we need is an entire and very swift reboot of every system in existence today: our energy systems, how we get around, how our factories are built and make the things we need and want, how we grow and produce our food — and what we produce. We really have to wipe the currently very dirty slate clean and start over, with zero emissions as our target. Of course, it's a very tall, if not impossible and idyllic, order and will be challenging especially for gen-next (but hey, they're the ones with the brains and the pizazz to make it happen!), but we already have systems we can put into place. We do have renewable energy sources (solar, wind and hydro-power), we are afforesting, rewilding and protecting wilderness areas, we are changing our eating habits (lesser fast food) and we've placed caps on carbon emissions which reduce every year. But alas, it's all happening far too slowly compared to the rate at which climate change and global warming are barrelling along.

Sitting, Not So Pretty!

Unfortunately, there is a status quo resistance to adapting these changes at the scale that is required. Big industrialists are not willing to ditch dirty energy (with which they are so pally) and often have political backing; we as consumers are not willing to change our own habits, especially

if we are comfortable as expense. Governments —
— are not willing to, or to, play along at the scale nations willing to extend reduce their emissions to are pillaging them further most countries continue to are actively searching and fuels. The filthy rich continue over everyone with their A tiny fraction of people more carbon than entire hey, those tiny fraction of off to get where they are, they've stashed away in The point is that if everyone there would be

we are, albeit at someone else's especially of developing countries say they don't have the resources required, and nor are developed enough help to these countries to the required levels; some in fact of their natural resources. And use dirty energy regardless, and drilling to extract even more fossil to flaunt their wealth and trample Godzilla-sized carbon footprints. consume more resources and emit nations do. You could argue that people probably worked their butts and so deserve every bar of gold Switzerland, but that's not the point. on earth had the same goal in mind,

nothing left on earth
except toxic

fumes, crazy weather, calamitous floods, cracked-earth fields, bone-dry droughts and millions of skeletal refugees (human and animal) staggering around with gaunt eyes and hollow stomachs. That total reboot of the system is therefore needed like never before, to make our potpourri planet a place that even advanced aliens might consider worth colonizing or at least vacationing in! (Why do you think they've stayed away for so long?) Here's a sample of some of the rebooting we need to do:

The cement industry needs a complete makeover; we urgently need to change how we make concrete. If the cement industry was to be thought of as a country it would be the third largest emitter of carbon emissions in the world — and much of this concrete is being poured by China. Do we really need colossal infrastructure projects like big dams, which consume vast quantities of cement, when it's been proved time and again that big dams do not really deliver all they promise and in fact do far more damage than good?

Recently, in Wales, an Indian-owned steel plant and the UK government agreed to invest 1.25 billion pounds (500 million pounds as a grant from the government) in order to replace an old coke and coal burning open-cast steel plant with an electric arc furnace plant. The old steelworks was the United Kingdom's single biggest carbon emitter. Of the more than 8,000 workers employed, it is said that 5,000 will be retained. Naturally, one feels for the 3,000 whose jobs may be on the line but the move will reduce the United Kingdom's total carbon emissions by 1.5 per cent.

The cost of solar energy has reduced by over 80 per cent since just 2009, yet we are burning 80 per cent more coal now than we did in 2000. So solar energy is not replacing fossil fuels as it ought to be; it's just adding to the total amount of energy we use. And the need of the hour is energy substitution, not energy addition.

Drilling for oil and gas, and mining for coal carries on unabated: many countries say they have no choice but to use these dirty fuels: they need the power in order to develop. That is as may be, but it means we are bringing Armageddon just that little bit closer to us, so much sooner. Climate change and global warming are already barrelling into us – and all we can do at the moment is try to mitigate their destructive effects the best we can, which basically means physically running away from anticipated extreme weather disasters, be they hurricanes, floods, wildfires or droughts, which in turn cause massive social problems like the refugee crises being experienced in so many parts of the world. So many thousands of people have been evacuated from their homes – as even I was in danger of being, in 2023!

Yes, the internal combustion engine has been put on notice by many automobile manufacturers and nations (2030 is one deadline set by some), but we really need to put the pedal to the metal here. We need to reach a stage where we are assured of zero carbon emissions from every sphere of activity, be it deforestation, agriculture, waste disposal, breeding of livestock and of course transportation and construction. Of course, 'net zero' has been cited as the ultimate goal, but those goalposts are still very, very far away, and we're just crawling towards them.

If our potpourri planet could come together and form a 'global government' as one writer put it, or at least, put institutions into place that could chivvy us along briskly (and mandatorily) towards creating a self-sustaining world — with a time cap in addition to an emissions cap — maybe something could come out of it. The horribly fractious state of the world today doesn't seem to make that likely anytime soon (we're too busy fighting wars), and so many countries (especially the developed ones) have not even kept the promises they have made in past accords. But all of us, regardless of nationality or beliefs, will have to believe that a sustainable future is not only possible but is worth fighting for, and for that everyone will simply have to come together and pull their weight. It's simple: one country may be able to use the latest technology and be squeaky-clean, and even be net zero; another may still be going full throttle with the use of ancient dirty fossil fuel technology: it makes no difference to Mother Nature. Her heavy hand of retribution will sooner or later strike everyone.

A study done in 2018, revealed that India would suffer the most, among all countries in the world, from the consequences of climate change, global warming and extreme weather, thanks to its geographical location. We're the first in the firing line, which is why It is imperative that at least we go full throttle trying to straighten things up. (We are traversing at a pretty good clip, but the trot needs to be turned into a gallop!) But ultimately every ecosystem in the world will be affected, which in turn will affect every country in the world. It's like an ocean liner that has been holed at one end; the cabins at that end will go under first, but ultimately the whole ship will go down — just as the Titanic did.

And really, that would be one Titanic disaster too many.

There's an easy way to drive this point home: visit an open-cast coal mine, or a desperate drug-and-alcohol afflicted slum with cockroaches dropping into your hair, or a cement or iron ore plant, or New Delhi in the dead of winter, or even a glittering, frigidly air conditioned mall dazzling with steel and glass and dizzy boutiques. Then visit (if you can find it) a golden empty beach, miles long, (with not a plastic bag or bottle to be seen), a majestic mountain range, a patch of rainforest teeming and buzzing with kaleidoscopic life, a crystal-clear stream or river and air that is sharp, crisp and cool as a salad and that makes you lungs sing. There you have it: Armageddon or the Garden of Eden. The choice is yours.

CHAPTER 2: HOW TO MAKE BIG MAMA SMILE AGAIN

After reading all this so far you may want to throw up your hands and despairingly exclaim, 'But what can I do to make Big Mama (aka Mother Nature) smile again?' She's in a towering rage and furious with us, and is getting after us like some kind of manic hellcat. Well, for a start, she hasn't yet completely blown her stack with us, and God forbid she ever does, but there's a lot you can do to (literally) cool her down, even though it may take ages for her to fully forgive and forget.

You Have the Power: Use It!

Remember so many major environmental campaigns, conservation drives, clean-up acts etc. were started off by just one single person or a small group of people. They showed the same doggedness, ingenuity and perseverance as our space scientists did. People like Rachel Carson, Sir David Attenborough, MK Ranjitsinhji, Dr Salim Ali, Jane Goodall, Dian Fossey, Birute Galdikas, Greta Thunberg, Jacques Cousteau, Boyan Slat, Sonam Wangchuk,

Sunderlal Bahuguna, Melati and Isabel Wisjen, Afroz Shah and so many, many more. These happily are not even the tip of the tip of the iceberg! They made the rest of us sit up and take notice – and even take action and change our habits. They wrote in the papers, rallied in the streets, screamed and yelled, got arrested, tramped for miles on foot to check ground realities, gave up on hamburgers and cheesecake, planted trees and even forests... They are people like you or I: some are students simply outraged by what they saw was happening, some are scientists who devoted their entire careers to their cause (it could be studying a nondescript little frog or amphibian, or lions and whales). They are groups of citizens who realized that the legacy they (and all of us) were leaving behind was something their children and grandchildren would never forgive them for. They include anyone who wanted to be able to take in a breath of fresh air, without coughing like a chain smoker, or a sip of water without suffering from stomach cramps. And once they found their cause, they stuck to it with bulldog tenacity for the rest of their lives, refusing to back down.

And all too often the forces they were up against were formidable: industrialists and businesspeople with heavy artillery, capacious pockets, concrete consciences and zero scruples, backed up by politicians most interested in their own personal and obscenely grand 'welfare' schemes, to hell with the rest of us. But some of the rest of us at least are not taking this lying down, and today, thanks to the relentless drive of these conscientious objectors' efforts, the tide is just beginning to turn. Admittedly because Big Mama has begun showing that she too has a heavy hand, heavier than anything her enemies can counter with. And also because once the politicians realize that what most people want is a thriving, humming rainforest — rather than a monstrous dam which will drown those same forests (killing every living thing in them), garrot rivers and silt up to the hilt within a few years, and make everyone's life miserable — they will know that they may well lose their precious votes. Then they'll do what they do best: cross over! But yes, for that to happen you and I (and even honest Casca out there!) will have to put our shoulders to the wheel.

We all live pretty crazy lives these days, what with multitasking, swotting for ferociously competitive (and frankly inhumane) professional exams, raising families, working 24X7, looking at our smartphones every ten seconds, battling rabid traffic, juggling with toddlers under one arm and laptops in the other, all at the same time. So, who has the time for environmental causes? It seems a lot of people do, and that could include you. Like in everything else, maybe it's best to start off simply: cut your carbon footprint as much as possible, do not waste (but do segregate your waste), and discourage it when you see it happen, check the sources of your food, avoid plastic as far as possible and so on. You don't really have to go out on the streets and scream and wave placards if you find that is difficult or embarrassing — though the more of you that do the better for the cause.

But there are simpler ways, many of which we have been lectured to, ad infinitum. Take your own bags when you go shopping. Use public transport wherever possible. Take your own stainless steel flask of water wherever you go.

The continued wholesale use of plastic bottles and plastic bags just staggers me. At any public function or private party, the arena will be strewn with plastic bottles. So many restaurants still offer water in plastic bottles in the same manner they offer you a bottle of their finest wine. Sportspeople who need to be regularly hydrated open plastic bottles by the dozen. I loved the Big Bang Theory series but was appalled by the number of times the actors opened their fridges and casually took out a plastic water bottle for a drink (and occasionally were depicted throwing perfectly good food into the trashcan for really no reason)! That mentality needs to change before it seeps into our psyche. Not so long ago, we got Coke and Limca and milk in glass bottles, which we had to return to get refills, or refunds if we didn't want refills. It didn't kill us or take years off our lives! Our thinking needs to be changed.

When the Metro first started in Delhi, back in 2002, it wasn't very popular (and people were scared of the escalators). When I took my first ride from home to Connaught Place, I was pleasantly surprised – the journey took around eight minutes (as against thirty minutes by car). This was so cool, I thought, but as I exited, I frowned. The Exit (and Entrance) gate I used had taken up a part of the parking lot where I usually parked my car. Where the heck was I supposed to park now? Then the light bulb went on! Hey, I wouldn't now have to use my car to come here anymore, forget about having to park it! And driving (and parking) in Delhi is only for the insane. It just shows: if there is a better, quicker, cleaner, cooler more practical alternative to private cars, people will pick it – as lakhs of daily commuters in Delhi now do.

Cycling has often been touted as one way to reduce your carbon footprint while getting around. It's become hugely popular in many European cities, like Amsterdam for example. Yes, we have the weather as an issue here — though this can be circumvented by designing biking paths under canopies of trees. Many people have begun commuting by bicycles, though given our total lack of traffic sense, or decency, this could be hazardous in the extreme. Tracks/paths dedicated to cycles could surely be built to deal with this issue.

Want Not, Waste Not; Why Not, Buy Not!

There are other small and relatively painless ways in which we can do our bit. Many restaurants pile your plate with helpings which are far too large (or maybe I have a far too small appetite!). Yes, there are those which serve minuscule helpings which consist more of silly, frilly decorations than actual food, which is anyway usually inedible! So, either you stuff yourself to the gills (and burp the rest of the day) or leave what you can't eat on your plate — which again will gnaw at your conscience for the

rest of the day and cause indigestion. (Do ask for a doggy-bag in such instances!) Restaurants should really serve you as much as you want. Many eating establishments and hotels claim that they give the leftovers of their buffets to the poor and needy. The packed meals you get on airlines and the railways are another source of tremendous waste. Let's say an airline orders 20,000 packed meals a day to serve on its various flights around the world. If even just 10 per cent of the food in each tray is wasted it would amount to 2,000 wasted meals – and ones you could not give to anyone else, except maybe to animals.

Resorts at hill stations often just dump their garbage (as do tourists) down the mountainside. I once spent a holiday knee-deep at one such garbage heap, waiting for paradise flycatchers to come swooping down at my feet virtually, to pick up the flies that buzzed around it. But yes, if you encounter something like this, do raise a stink – in the lobby, where the most people can hear you! If you want to be militant, pick some of it up and dump it on the receptionist's counter!

Like it or not we live in a consumer society, where shopping madly is what keeps the economy ticking. The more stuff you buy, the more of it has to be made, the more factories you need and the more people you need to give jobs to in order to manufacture all that stuff, and sadly the more smoke those factories belch out, and the more electricity and water they use. The best way to help the environment would be to shop wisely. Don't buy so much food that more than half of it goes to waste. Do you really need twenty-five pairs of jeans or six-dozen T-shirts? Or 200 pairs of shoes? (You can only wear one at a time and you have only two feet).

Here I can gleefully put my hand up to be counted! My sisters and girlfriends, who usually buy all my clothes for me, despair: 'You're still wearing that ancient T-shirt — throw it out, it looks like a jharan! It must be twenty-five years old at least, it should be in a museum!' Well, there's really nothing wrong with the shirt. Maybe it's a little jaded, but it is so comfortable, so why do I need six more? And throw it out? Cannot do! And also, I hate shopping for clothes!

May Jugaad Rule!

What's worse is that we're beginning to suffer from the 'throw-away' syndrome, like what the West has been afflicted with since forever. A gadget breaks down, and it is instantly replaced. A new gadget (smartphones come to mind instantly) comes out and we have to upgrade, otherwise there's egg on our face and what will people think? And manufacturers pounce on this like great white sharks. 'Built-in-obsolescence' is their mantra. What's worse is that sometimes they strong-arm you into buying something you don't really have to.

I had a perfectly good printer recently, made by a leading manufacturer. Yes, the ink cartridges cost a bomb (they'll sell the printer cheap, but rip you off with the cartridges), but it worked flawlessly. Then the cartridges were discontinued: so perforce I had to buy a new printer because either I scoured the jugaad market for fake old cartridges (which sooner or later would make a mess of the printer) or else remained printer-less. So, the perfectly good old printer will eventually be junked and find its way contributing to some of the millions of tons of unnecessary plastic waste we create every year. And so much for the manufacturer's concerns about the environmental damage it was causing thanks to its policies. This is where big industries – who can afford to behave better – rile the heck out of me, and should rile you too. They need to be taken to task – through legislation if necessary. Troll them!

I've been told that I should really get a new TV set; actually, they say, these days you ought to replace your sets every two or three years. The one I have was bought back in 2005, before all these smart sets came around, flaunting their flatscreens and whatnot. Well sure enough, recently the old set's speakers gave up. The set was long out of production so getting the speaker replaced was not an option. But yes, I had an old CD player that had also given up the ghost, but whose speakers were just fine. My house-help, who is a wizard at jugaad, simply fitted the old CD player's speakers to the TV and hey presto, we were back in business!

The packaging industry is another huge source of often unsustainable waste. Everything you buy these days comes in hermetically sealed industrial strength plastic. Sometimes it makes you think that the packaging cost more than the product itself. There's a simple way of getting your message across. Unpack the article in the shop and leave the packaging on the shop counter, because you do not need the dabba! If enough people do this, the message should get back to the manufacturer sooner than later via the exasperated shop-owner! If you're moving house, professional packers will pack every item – be it a fork or a spoon – separately, much of which is unnecessary. Bubble-wrap has come as a boon to the packaging industry – but no matter how much fun it is to pop the 'bubbles', it is made of plastic and there's so much of it being used that a lot eventually ends up in landfills or the oceans, where it remains. So, try using old newspaper, old clothes and rags and any other reusable stuffing you can find. In the old days, when we had to move house, stuff was packed in wooden crates (reusable), and straw was the stuffing that was used (and I still remember, how nice it smelt!).

Muckraking!

Whether you're a school student, in college or an ordinary citizen, you will have occasionally been called up for 'clean-up drives' or 'tree-planting drives', usually at the behest of some leader or politically motivated group. Clean-up drives happen regularly every year, and every year the mess that needs to be cleaned up, if anything, is bigger and more stinky and disgusting than ever. Before you agree to take part in these, you must bug the organizers and ask them what they've done since last year to plug the sources of all the muck that they are now asking you to wade through and pick up? Why is muck being replaced by yet more muck? Year after year.

But there have been successful clean-up drives which have led to major changes in attitude among the aam janta and even governments. Appalled by the filth on Mumbai's Versova beach, Afroz Shah, an environmental activist and lawyer, along with an eighty-four-year-old companion, in October 2015 began picking up the trash, piece by piece. For six to eight weeks their efforts were ignored, then they were joined by a couple more men. In three years, it became a major movement, involving

60,000 students, fisherfolk, film stars, politicians, citizen's groups, schoolchildren, slum-dwellers et al., resulting in a beach where Olive Ridley turtles have come back to breed. The group is now setting their sights at cleaning up Mumbai's stinking Mithi river (and refuge of flamingos) and choked mangrove forests. The infection has spread country-wide. This story always makes me smile: it reminds me of that old prank where one person would suddenly stop in the middle of the street, and look up intently at the sky (at absolutely nothing), soon to be joined by another and then another (all murmuring wondrously at each other and pointing at nothing!), and before you knew it the whole mohalla would have joined them! But here, for such a genuine cause!

On the island of Bali (which produced 330,000 tonnes of plastic waste annually) two sisters, Melati and Isabel Wisjen, then aged just ten and twelve years old, regarded the discarded plastic bags strewn about everywhere as an issue. They began a movement, 'Bye-Bye Plastic Bags', involving youngsters and using social media and door-to-door campaigning to discourage and ban the use of plastic bags on their island. A petition to the governor containing 10,000 signatures was sent in 2015, asking for a ban, but was ignored. In 2017 the sisters went on a hunger strike, which immediately caught the attention of the media — and woke up the governor. In 2018 a legislation was signed banning the use of plastic bags and Styrofoam. The girls were fourteen and sixteen years old by then.

Back in 2011, Boyan Slat an eighteen-year-old Dutch engineering student devised and designed a huge net, scoop and funnel system, that was to be set afloat around the Great Pacific Garbage Patch to scoop and suck up — and even sort out — as much of the floating plastic garbage as it could. He started the non-profit organization 'The Ocean Clean Up' in 2013 for the purpose. There were many technical setbacks that had to be overcome, but by 2021, as much as 9,000 kilograms of trash was being removed and treated. A new system called 'The Interceptor' was devised, which is a solar-powered barge like contraption, scalable and to be stationed at the mouths of rivers (1,000 of all the world's rivers are responsible for 80 per cent of the oceans' plastic pollution) to catch the plastic before it entered the oceans. By 2022 Interceptors had been deployed by Indonesia, Malaysia, the Dominican Republic and Vietnam, with several other countries (including India, though far down the line) in the queue.

Every Sapling, a Child

As for tree planting drives — these are conducted occasionally to compensate for trees hacked down elsewhere, or as part of 'afforestation' drives or by visiting bigwigs to sacred locations such as Rajghat in New Delhi. But what's in place to ensure that the delicate sapling that you (or even a prime minister) planted has a future and won't be eaten by goats? Most just wither and die — maintenance (of virtually everything) has always been our great Achilles' heel and shows a complete lack of responsibility. You need to visit your sapling regularly and kick up a shindig if you think it is (and the others planted alongside are) being neglected or molested. But again, these afforestation drives can work. We've seen what individuals can do, growing forests in wastelands.

Becoming a Mover and Shaker

If you feel strongly enough you can join — or form — your own environmental group or NGO. Again, many of the world's best-known NGOs like the WWF were started by one or two individuals or a small group of passionate people and now have a presence and influence around the world. If you are really ambitious, you can even join politics to push your environmental agenda. Global warming and climate change are becoming big-ticket and very hot political issues these days — and are on the top of the agendas of many international conferences and meetings. At the United Nations General Assembly Meeting held in September 2023, it was right up there with the Ukraine war among the top two topics up for discussion. And it's always good to have the big guns of the government on your side, because then you can really achieve results on the ground.

All Hail Nosy Parkers!

If you are naturally curious, research and development could be the way you could put your shoulder to the wheel. Mother Nature still holds myriad secrets from us — there is so much we still don't know and have to discover. (We have only explored 5 per cent of the world's deep oceans, though maybe this is a good thing!) It has been research and development that has enabled the price of solar energy to drop as precipitously as it has, that has improved the way we grow our food, made our automobiles more fuel efficient and less polluting, and that has led to the protection of rainforests and other ecosystems. If scientists hadn't studied or researched ecosystems like rainforests, wetlands, oceans, coral beds and even deserts, we would not have had a clue as to how important they are in the larger scheme of things and why it is essential to preserve them. The same holds true for the study of so many species of animals, plants, bacteria, viruses and fungi and their role in keeping planet earth ticking over nicely. In innumerable instances of course, we have taken our cues from Mother Nature to improve upon technologies. The upturned wing-tips you see on modern aircraft, which improve aerodynamic efficiency and consequently reduce fuel consumption and therefore the amount of emissions, were 'inspired' from the upturned flight pinions of soaring eagles and vultures. We're now even trying to develop a synthetic chlorophyll substitute. We're dabbling in bio- and genetic-engineering, and trying our best to crack the biggest mystery of all: life.

The media provides another huge outlet – with vast reach. Whether it is journalism or social media, the making of reels or full-fledged documentaries, the scope is limitless. You change one person's worldview and you will have achieved your goal (though of course it's nicer if you can change the worldview of the entire world!).

Bite the Bait!

All you need is curiosity; to be interested in life around you. Get immersed in whatever tickles your fancy (there is no shortage of subjects) and you'll have a lifetime's work and probably adventure laid out before you and certainly a very interesting life too. Jane Goodall was interested in chimpanzees as a child, and then managed to wangle her way (through the good offices of

Dr Louis Leakey, the anthropologist) to the Congo jungles, where she studied the animals (and discovered they could use tools) for all of her career. Gerald Durrell was fascinated by animals since childhood and went on to create his own zoo and the Jersey Preservation Trust, whose mandate was to captively breed animals on the brink of extinction (in the hope that they would eventually be ready to be repatriated to their original habitats). Dr Salim Ali got interested in birds after shooting an unusual sparrow, which eventually led to him (along with others) saving the Keoladeo National Park and Silent Valley from meeting a dreadful fate – and he became the country's leading ornithologist. Romulus Whitaker ensured that crocodiles didn't go extinct in India by successfully captive-breeding them. Kailash Sankhala got Project Tiger off and running. It is heartwarming to find that so many living creatures – be they insects, reptiles, amphibians, birds, mammals, plants, fungi or even bacteria – have at least one human guardian angel or patron saint, studying them, looking after their interests and well-being and screaming blue murder on their behalf.

We Were All Born Barefoot!

There's another major reason why we really need to get involved with nature and, by automatic default, become her protector. Like it or not we were born to walk barefoot on the earth, not in stilettos or hobnails on polished marbled floors. Spend three hours strolling around a gleaming glittering mall full of marble, glass, steel and chromium and tinned, frigid air and you will emerge glazed and glassy-eyed and robotic and in a hurry to get out of the air conditioning, no matter how hot it is outside. Spend those same three hours in the wilderness — a forest, riverside, meadow, woodland, savannah, mountainside, stream, waterfall, beach, ocean — or in the company of animals or birds, and you'll come back intoxicated, your eyes sparkling, a spring in your step, your blood humming happily in your veins (even if you've been bitten or stung!) and your heart joyous.

When I was a child there was no need for my parents to yell, 'Now go outside and play!' because we were for the most part already outside, raising hell! We got muddy, we got wet, we got sweaty, we got bitten and stung, we got bruised (because we had fallen out of a tree, maybe) and black-eyed, but we had to be chased back home, where we eventually returned with shining eyes and occasionally some ghastly creepy-crawly or rescued furry creature in our cupped palms. We lived in a real, living, breathing, pulsating world, in the environment we were meant for, not a make-believe, synthetic, virtual one where we spent the whole day staring glassy-eyed at flickering screens and manically thumb-punching buttons. You emerge from such a world feeling somehow hollowed out, your heart empty.

I really believe that children and young people have an instinct to naturally gel with nature: they know instinctively how to go about things in the outdoors. I've watched so many of the survival in the wild programs on TV (like the ones by Bear Grylls, for example), and so many times have shrugged and said, 'Well, what's so great about that, we knew that at age four!' For example, while climbing a wall or cliff or up a narrow shute, one of the cardinal rules is that you must have 'three points of contact' on the surface at all times. Well, every child knows that. We did the

dangerous 'chimney climb' up narrow spaces all the time (usually barefoot), without ever having to be instructed. Outdoors was where the real adventures and challenges lay; outdoors was the real schoolroom. Yes, modern technology can prevent children from getting into trouble, by say identifying a venomous snake or dangerous wasp on Google, but first you have to be outdoors to encounter any such creature!

Big Mama Therapist

In fact, for troubled kids (those involved in petty crime, anti-social activities, vandalism, drug or alcohol addiction), 'wilderness therapy' is being touted as one way to help them find their bearings. They're taken out into the wilds and made to team up and face several challenges – hiking long distances cross-country, cliff-climbing or descending, lighting a fire, swimming across rivers, gelling as a team, leading a team, setting up camp, finding (and cooking) food and water, building shelters for the night and so on. By the end of it, many are happier and fitter for it.

But really, look at us today! When the Air Quality Index shoots up and the sky is dirty-brown, children are forbidden from going outside to play. We're warned not to exercise or take part in sports, especially early in the morning, and to wear masks. Frankly we're being denied the most basic, fundamental right of all: to breathe in clean air, really to live!

While on an early morning walk recently, I suddenly realized one thing: oh yes, I would say that I'm interested in the well-being of the environment and so on and so forth, but invariably, in animated conversations with friends would begin by declaiming, 'They should do this, and they should do that!' The 'they' were never clearly defined and remained some vague invisible entity (usually an enemy), like the anonymous phantoms that work in musty government offices or for institutions, or our leaders who are protected from us by a bristling forest of gun-barrels. Oh-oh, so maybe that should be corrected to 'We should do this, and we should do that!' And who's the 'we'? Okay, so maybe it should really be, 'I should do this and I should do that!' That made me stop short! Yes, but of course... Maybe that's also why I wrote this book.

Years ago, my sister sent me this four-line story written by a little boy:

Once there was a lion
He ate everyone up
Then he ate himself up
The End

We have to make sure we don't eat ourselves up.

AFTERWORD

Much has happened since I finished writing this book in 2023. Unfortunately, we've been backpedalling instead of making positive moves to rein in global warming. The recent COP29 meet at Baku (November 2024) did not go as well as expected, with the Global North refusing to allocate more funds for the climate finance deal. The Global South nations, India among the loudest, demanded $1.3 trillion to transition to a greener way of development instead of the promised $300 billion by 2035.

At the United Nations-led Global Plastic Treaty Negotiations held in Busan in November 2024, India, among other nations, did not agree to a proposed cap on the production of primary plastic polymers (which are a major pollutant), citing a need for technical and financial assistance to manage plastic waste and that such a cap could impact its right to development.

In India, we've opened up for auction vast areas around the Nicobar Islands for mineral and oil exploration. The forthcoming political dispensation in the United States might bode ill for global warming, with plans to increase the use and excavation of fossil fuels and, at times, even blind denial that global warming is a reality.

But all need not seem lost. Once upon a time, the population of the Indian lion was down to just around twelve animals. With strict protection (initially by the Nawab of Junagadh), their numbers are now over 600. Mama Nature seems to be a lot like us: stroke her ego, cajole and cosset her a bit, and willy-nilly she'll bounce back with all her smiling benevolence. That's what we have to do now!

Ranjit Lal
December 2024

ABOUT THE AUTHOR

Ranjit Lal is the author of around fifty books — fiction and non-fiction — for children and adults who are children. His abiding interest in natural history, conversation, birds, animals and insects is reflected in many of his books. He was awarded the Zeiss Wildlife Lifetime Conservation Award for 2019. His books have won many awards, including the Crossword Award for Children's Writing, the Ladli National Media Award for Gender Sensitivity, the Crossword Raymond Award for Children's Writing and others. The Battle for Number 19 has been optioned for a film. His other interests include photography, automobiles, reading and cooking. He lives in Delhi.

ABOUT THE ILLUSTRATOR

Anushua Sinha is an illustrator who brings stories to life in unexpected ways. Trained as an architect in Mumbai, she quickly discovered that drawing floor plans wasn't nearly as thrilling as doodling environmentalist owls and banana dinosaurs and people actually pay for that! A graduate of the Savannah College of Art and Design, she focuses on editorial and children's book illustrations, often weaving themes of environmentalism into her work. Recognized by *3x3 Magazine, Creative Quarterly*, and the *Society of Illustrators of Los Angeles*, Anushua's art is filled with warmth and heart, making life and her work—a colorful adventure.

ACKNOWLEDGEMENTS

A warm thank you to Jaya Bhattacharji Rose for sweet-talking me into doing this book!

To Anushua, whose vibrant and lively illustrations have lifted it out of the morass of sludge it might otherwise have been.

To Ankita, who smoothened out the pothole-ridden prose and gross overwriting to leave an easy-to-read manuscript in her wake.

ALSO BY RANJIT LAL

Budgie, Bridge and Big Djinn

They form a formidable team: 14-year-old Budgie, out-spoken to a fault; Bridge, a steady teenager with a rocky past; and Big Djinn, the ferocious Tibetan Mastiff-German Shepherd mixed breed. Together they set about getting their own back on a gang of mean-spirited bird-watching bullies. That's the easy part. When faced with a terrifying, life-threatening situation, that endangers the very existence of their idyllic mountain home, they have to dig deep to find the courage and tenacity to deal with it... and face an enemy who will stop at nothing to get his own way. A thrilling adventure story that also brings forth the perils of environmental degradation.